A GUIDE TO NEW MEXICO FILM LOCATIONS

I0811489

A GUIDE TO
N
MEXI
FILM
JASON STRYKOWSKI

W

CO

LOCATIONS

From Billy the Kid
to *Breaking Bad* and Beyond

University of New Mexico Press Albuquerque

© 2021 by Jason Strykowski
All rights reserved. Published 2021
Printed in the United States of America

ISBN 978-0-8263-6297-1 (paper)
ISBN 978-0-8263-6298-8 (electronic)

Library of Congress Control Number: 2021942365

Founded in 1889, the University of New Mexico sits on the traditional homelands of the Pueblo of Sandia. The original peoples of New Mexico—Pueblo, Navajo, and Apache—since time immemorial have deep connections to the land and have made significant contributions to the broader community statewide. We honor the land itself and those who remain stewards of this land throughout the generations and also acknowledge our committed relationship to Indigenous peoples. We gratefully recognize our history.

COVER ILLUSTRATION: Highway near Santa Fe New Mexico © 2018 Jim Ekstrand | istockphoto.com; Rio Grande Gorge Bridge © 2021 Mindy Basinger Hill; White Sands © FiledIMAGE | istockphoto.com.
DESIGNED BY Mindy Basinger Hill
COMPOSED IN Chapparral Pro and Mr Eaves Mod OT

CONTENTS

PART VI. SOUTHERN NEW MEXICO

PART VII. ADDITIONAL DESTINATIONS

INTRODUCTION

Since the early days of film, New Mexico has hosted hundreds of productions. This book showcases the diverse locations used throughout the state, from the Bisti Badlands to the Old Main State Penitentiary.

New Mexico has been a desirable Western landscape since the early twentieth century. Films like *Cowboy*, *Billy Jack*, *True Grit*, *Death Valley*, and dozens of other titles used the spare desert for adventure and intrigue. That started to change in the 1960s with *Lonely are the Brave*. The film featured Kirk Douglas as an old cowboy shooing away modern society. It not only featured Western locations but also urban areas, including a stream of traffic on Route 66 near Albuquerque. The movie showed what modern-day producers see in New Mexico: unique landscapes like White Sands National Monument and Spaceport America as well as the downtown centers of Las Cruces, Las Vegas, Santa Fe, Madrid, Deming, and Albuquerque, home of the *Breaking Bad* series.

Today, New Mexico is at the cusp of a new century in film. With leadership from Governor Michelle Lujan Grisham, New Mexico's film incentives are the most competitive in the United States. The state has welcomed production crews, actors, and other film crew with its ideal climate, which features more than three hundred days of sunshine.

Producers used to come to New Mexico because it fit the script. Today, they come for the year-round high-quality production environment, the many locations, and the professional studios and stages that can suit any story.

Alicia J. Keyes CABINET SECRETARY / NEW MEXICO ECONOMIC DEVELOPMENT

SITE LOCATIONS

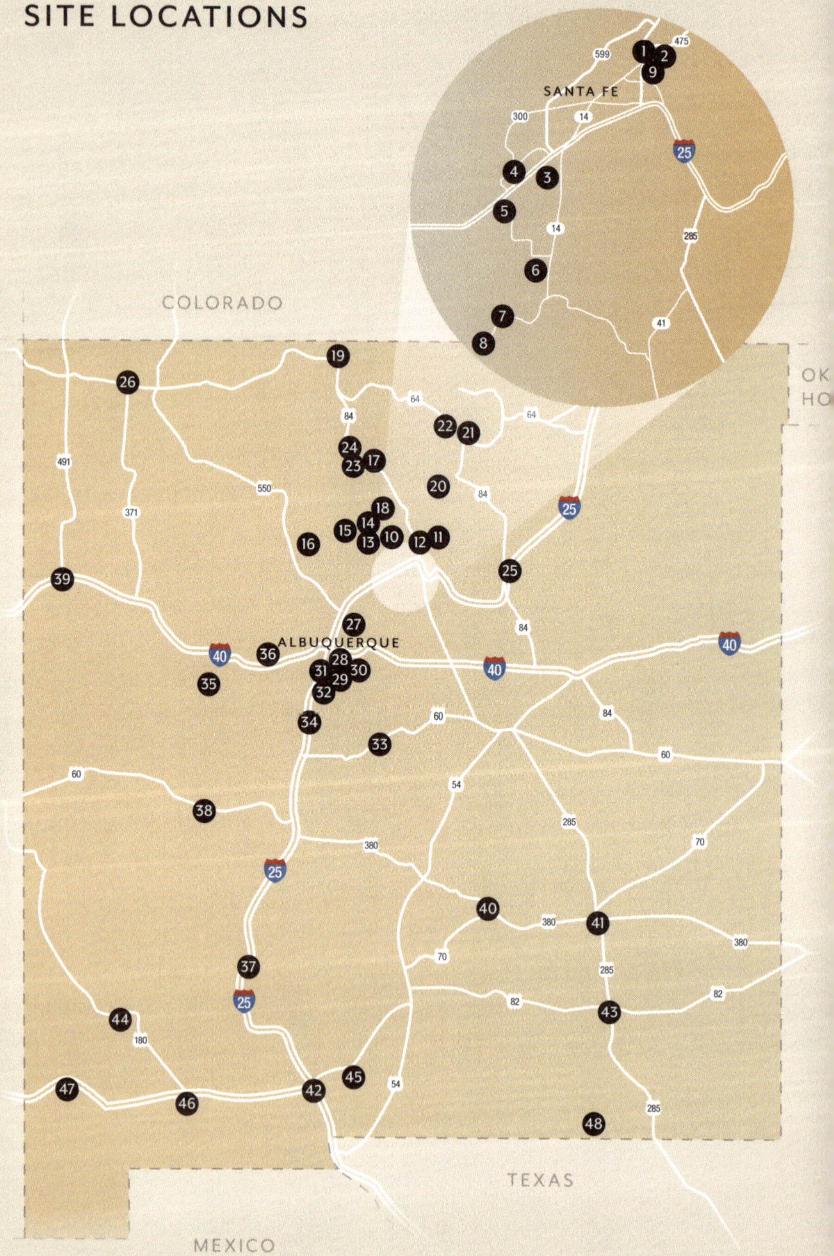

1 Santa Fe Plaza and Downtown Santa Fe
2 Santa Fe Like a Film Local
3 Old Main State Penitentiary
4 El Rancho de las Golondrinas
5 Bonanza Creek Ranch
6 W. Eaves Movie Ranch
7 Cerrillos
8 Madrid
9 Evangelo's Cocktail Lounge
10 Diablo Canyon
11 Ski Santa Fe
12 Tesuque Village and Pueblo
13 Bandelier National Monument
14 Los Alamos and Environs
15 Valles Caldera National Preserve
16 Gilman Tunnels and Fenton Lake
17 Plaza Blanca and Abiquiú
18 Puye Cliffs and Santa Clara Pueblo
19 Cumbres & Toltec Scenic Railroad (CTSRR)
20 Truchas and the High Road to Taos
21 Taos Pueblo
22 Rio Grande Gorge Bridge
23 Rio Chama and Abiquiú Dam & Lake
24 Ghost Ranch
25 Las Vegas
26 Farmington
27 Sandia Mountains
28 *Breaking Bad* and *Better Call Saul* in Albuquerque
29 Downtown Albuquerque
30 Albuquerque Like a Film Local
31 Albuquerque Rail Yards
32 Isleta Pueblo
33 Mountainair and Environs
34 Belen
35 Acoma Pueblo
36 To'hajiilee
37 Truth or Consequences and the New Mexico Spaceport
38 Very Large Array (VLA)
39 Gallup
40 Lincoln and Ruidoso
41 Roswell
42 Las Cruces
43 Artesia
44 Silver City
45 White Sands
46 Deming
47 Lordsburg and Environs
48 Carlsbad Caverns

A LOCATIONS SCOUT TELLS ALL

Like many other forward-thinking entrepreneurs and artists of the time, my family migrated to New Mexico in the 1930s. They hoped to escape economic depression and find new opportunity for expression in a land of light and clarity. New Mexico has historically been known as the perfect artist's palette. With similar artistic aspirations, early filmmakers were drawn to the dramatic locations found in New Mexico's high desert plateau.

Filmmakers continue to be drawn to the wide variety of locations New Mexico has to offer, from gritty truck stops to pristine wilderness and residential locations in the lowest to highest income brackets; from contemporary architectural masterpieces to humble adobe homes; barrios to boardrooms; crack houses to castles; and mountain passes to muddy back alleys.

As a film scout, I have grown to appreciate the purity and honesty of New Mexican locations. They are sometimes breathtakingly beautiful, not always pretty, but always real. What you see is what you get.

Currently, economic incentives have brought many projects to New Mexico that don't need a place with character as much as they require a working environment with excellent infrastructure, crew, and government and public support. As a result New Mexico has been asked to stand in for other locales. I have been asked to show locations in New Mexico that could pose as Arizona, Colorado, Louisiana, Mexico, Nevada, Texas, Afghanistan, and other parts of the Middle East. These are perhaps not as big a stretch as shows that have filmed New Mexico as Berlin, Boston, Hawaii, Nairobi, New York, Philadelphia, Tehran, and the most unbelievable—Paris. The state is accommodating but not wholly comfortable with these kinds of dress-up games. She instead shines brightest as herself—an eclectic, multicultural, economically diverse, high desert masterpiece. New Mexico locations are strong enough to stand alone as their own characters in storytelling.

Many authors, both past and present, "get" New Mexico and have incorporated the state as its own unique place in their scripts. She can be a harsh and unforgiving background for Westerns both contemporary and classic. Or she can be a sleepy, dusty backdrop for that most human of stories. She offers a clarion, pristine sky filled with billowing clouds to envelope whatever an imagination has to illustrate.

But it isn't easy. If the ever-changing weather doesn't knock a production on its ass, then the blistering stillness will. Filmmaking in New Mexico is not for the faint of heart. And for the audiences who enjoy the end results, all are certain to share my affection for this most unique of locations.

Cyndy McCrossen LOCATIONS SCOUT

A NOTE ON FILMS AND TELEVISION SHOWS

Beginning in 1897, filmmakers have descended en masse to New Mexico. Thousands of films, television shows, and shorts have featured the state's dramatic landscape and its unique architecture. All in all, there have been far too many projects made in New Mexico to mention them all in this volume. Even the filmography in the back of this book is not intended to be comprehensive.

Prior to 2003, it was somewhat easier to keep track of New Mexico productions. The introduction of an incentive package by Governor Gary Johnson and the expansion made by Governor Bill Richardson ushered in an explosion in the craft. Similar programs in other states, as well as Canada, all but guaranteed an era of "runaway productions" in which studios moved their shows out of Los Angeles and sought rebates in other states and other countries. In New Mexico, the program proved so successful that almost every year since its beginning, hundreds of films have shot in the Land of Enchantment.

Alongside the explosion in Hollywood filmmaking, advancements in technology over the past thirty years opened up the medium for many. Digital film cameras became a viable and often inexpensive alternative to celluloid. Consumer editing programs made their way to the home computer. Today, most modern cell phones are capable of filming and editing. Consequently, taking full measure of all the films created and produced in New Mexico would be almost impossible.

In this book, I have focused on projects that are representative of a certain locations and on some films and television shows with avid fan bases. I've also tried to bring up films that I believe are worth watching or considering. I worked on many of the projects detailed in the following pages and bring them up because I have firsthand knowledge.

Ad for *Sundown* (1941). Courtesy of the Paul Andrew Hutton Collection and United Artists.

Lobby card for *The Rounders* (1965). Courtesy of the Paul Andrew Hutton Collection and Metro-Goldwyn Mayer.

If any of the New Mexico films or television shows you admire aren't mentioned by name, then I encourage you to research it on your own and use the template I've provided here to turn your interest into an experience. At the back of this book, you'll find some suggestions for further reading, which will give you a few of the tools to get started.

Lobby card for *Lonely are the Brave* (1962). Courtesy of the Paul Andrew Hutton Collection and Universal Pictures.

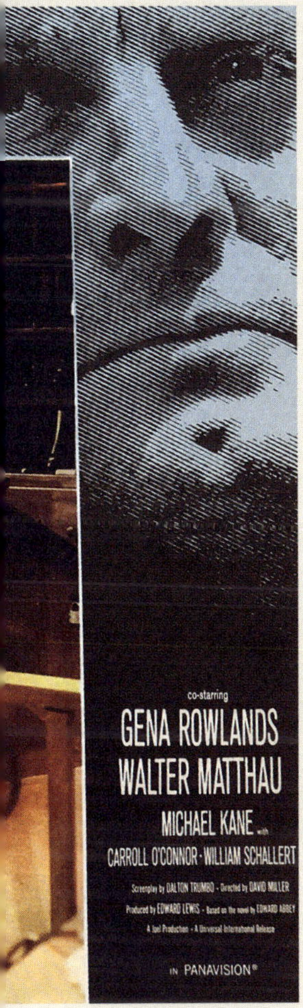

HOW TO USE THIS GUIDE

Production crew members usually receive a call sheet and a map prior to each day on set. The call sheet gives details on the day's work, including what pages of the script will be shot and which cast members are to be included. The map, of course, provides directions to the set. In New Mexico, that's not always so easy.

Consider this book your call sheet and map to New Mexico's shooting locations. In these pages you'll find your way to shooting destinations and discover information on each site's natural history, human past, and associated films and television shows. I've also dropped in some fun activities at each stop.

Each site also has a recommendation for a nearby hotel and restaurant. Many of the businesses listed are frequently used by film and television production companies. Others were suggested to me by New Mexico film workers.

If you're not sure what to see or where you're headed, check out the "For Fans of" section for some pointers.

Bite the Bullet, © 1975 (renewed 2003) by Columbia Pictures Industries, Inc. All Rights Reserved. Courtesy of Columbia Pictures and the Paul Andrew Hutton Collection.

WHAT TO BRING

Mike Ehrmantrout, the calculating enforcer in the *Breaking Bad* universe, keeps a "go bag" in his car at the airport. Most production personnel don't have stacks of cash in a duffle in their car, but they do have a gym bag filled with cold and hot weather gear and plenty of sunscreen. Here's what to pack for your New Mexico excursion.

The first essential is water. New Mexico is hot, dry, and high. Even in winter, it's easy to get dehydrated. Some of the sites in this book are remote and don't have running water on site, so bring water with you.

RED AND GREEN

In New Mexico, chile is spelled with an *e*, and it's everywhere. The Hatch green chile pepper is grown in Southern New Mexico, harvested, roasted, and then put in stew, hamburgers, burritos, and even beer. When dried, the pepper turns red and takes on a slightly stronger flavor. Usually, red pepper is ground. If you want both on your burrito, ask for "Christmas style."

In the summer, keep a hat around to make the strong sun tolerable. On set, many crew keep a shemagh, or keffiyeh, handy. These Arabian headdresses are great for keeping the dust and sun off your face. A sturdy pair of sunglasses is helpful too.

The late summer brings seasonal afternoon rain showers, locally called monsoons. A lightweight, waterproof jacket is useful to keep on hand, especially because conditions can change fast at high altitude.

LISTING CHANGES

We've carefully checked all the included businesses and activities, but things can change rapidly in New Mexico, and it's advisable to check ahead before making plans to travel. Some of the businesses included here are seasonal or run by families and may be subject to shifting schedules.

New Mexico is often confused for its more populous neighbor, Arizona, but you won't find a single saguaro cactus in the Land of Enchantment, and it's much colder in the winter. Be aware that Northern New Mexico is often below freezing in the winter. Warm clothes should also have a place in your "go bag."

If you're planning on hiking, a backpack and a first-aid kit are mandatory. Maybe throw some antacids in the kit should the green chile in town be a little hot.

PART I

FOR FANS OF

Assembling in *Marvel Studios' The Avengers* (2012).
Courtesy of Marvel Studios.

BLOCKBUSTER FILMS

The modern blockbuster period began in the 1970s, marked by the arrival of *Jaws* and then *Star Wars: A New Hope*. The minds behind these films worked together on *Indiana Jones and the Last Crusade*, which shot on the Cumbres & Toltec Scenic Railroad (C&TSRR) (see location 19). Steven Spielberg (*Jaws*) directed this third film in the Indiana Jones tetralogy, while George Lucas (*Star Wars*) produced it.

Although Harrison Ford was not in the opening scene of *Indiana Jones and the Last Crusade*, which filmed on the C&TSRR, he appeared in New Mexico for the tentpole, sci-fi mashup *Cowboys & Aliens*. Ford matches wits in the film with Daniel Craig, taking a break from his role as James Bond. Craig plays Jake Lonergan, a plainsman struggling with amnesia. As he and Ford are coming to blows, the aliens arrive in the heart of the Western town at Bonanza Creek Ranch (see location 5).

Jon Favreau, hot on the heels of his success with *Iron Man*, directed *Cowboys & Aliens*. A few years later he was one of the producers on *Marvel Studios' The Avengers*. The film was not only the biggest blockbuster made in New Mexico, but one of the highest-grossing films of all time. The production used the Albuquerque Rail Yards (see location 31) as a secondary studio, and a small section of New York City was built inside.

Christian Bale put down his Batman costume to come to New Mexico and fight androids in *Terminator Salvation*. The fourth film in the Terminator franchise was shot throughout the state, including a thrilling aerial battle scene over the Rio Grande Gorge Bridge (see location 22).

WESTERN FILMS

The real-life Billy the Kid engineered his most famous escape in Lincoln (see location 40). The small town has changed little since Billy fought his way out of the courthouse and is a must for fans of both the real and fictional Wild West.

Among the many screen renditions of Billy's life, *Young Guns* transformed Cerrillos (see location 7) into a rough approximation of Lincoln. Cerrillos is also steeped in its own authentic nineteenth-century mining history.

Not far from Cerrillos, the J. W. Eaves Movie Ranch (see location 6) was a real working cattle ranch until a Western television show arrived. Only a few years later, Eaves was transformed into a nineteenth-century facsimile town, and it has since hosted scores of Westerns.

The red rock cliffs and year-round flow of the Rio Chama (see location 23) give the river a timeless look that Westerns adore. Equally as striking, the white formations at Plaza Blanca (see location 17) are a frequently used backdrop for Westerns.

The Lincoln County Courthouse, ca. 1933. Courtesy the Historic American Buildings Survey and Wikimedia Commons.

Dennis Hopper, Peter Fonda, and Jack Nicholson in *Easy Rider*, © 1969 (renewed 1997) by Columbia Pictures Industries, Inc. All Rights Reserved. Courtesy of Columbia Pictures and the Paul Andrew Hutton Collection.

INDIE FILMS

It wasn't simply that director and writer Herbert Biberman couldn't work in the studio system, he was actively blacklisted from it as a result of the House Un-American Activities Committee findings. To make a movie about striking miners near Silver City (see location 44), Biberman founded his own production company and flew against the Hollywood establishment, making him one of the first motion-picture filmmakers to come to New Mexico without studio backing.

When it hit theaters in 1969, *Easy Rider* challenged the heart of the studio system. On a modest budget, Dennis Hopper made a countercultural masterpiece that portrayed a different vision of the 1960s. Instead of the glossy image of the United States that other period films espoused, *Easy Rider*'s America was grubby and dirty, a vision that Hopper captured with a relatively small crew and a grab-and-go style of filmmaking that constantly teetered on the brink of disaster. Ultimately, the film went on to gross some $60 million dollars at the box office. It shot partially in Taos Pueblo (see location 21).

After the success of *Easy Rider*, Hollywood execs opened their hearts and wallets to offbeat films with a countercultural vibe. Monte Hellman, who had previously directed a number of Westerns starring pre-fame Jack Nicholson, got the go ahead to make his own road trip flick in *Two-Lane Blacktop*. Hellman cast musicians in the lead roles. James Taylor and the Beach Boys' Dennis Wilson say relatively little, but they own the road and the screen. Taylor picks a fight with a local racer at a burger joint in Santa Fe (see location 2).

At about the same time, actor Tom Laughlin brought his ideas about independent film and independent living to Santa Fe and Bandelier National Monument (see location 13). The film *Billy Jack* went in and out of studio hands, but it was Laughlin himself who ultimately figured out how best to distribute the film. His experiments with a wide, “four-wall” (or fully booked theater) release of the film paid huge dividends. The film was a hit.

Some decades later, director Allison Anders, a rising star in Hollywood, brought *Gas Food Lodging* to Deming (see location 46). Star Fairuza Balk won an Independent Spirit Award for her acting in this film.

FILM HISTORY

Only a few years after they invented a primitive motion-picture camera, employees of the Edison Manufacturing Company arrived at Isleta Pueblo (see location 32) to record students at the local school. The result was *Indian Day School*, the first motion picture made in New Mexico.

Just over a decade later, pioneering filmmakers made Las Vegas, New Mexico (see location 25), the studio hub of the Southwest. Romaine Fielding and Tom Mix shot reel after reel of silent film here, a few of which still survive. Both men were early stars of the medium.

Neither could compete with D. W. Griffith for fame, though. Griffith shot *A Pueblo Legend* at Isleta a few years before he forever

Director/actor Tom Mix (1919). Courtesy of the Library of Congress.

changed film history with *The Birth of a Nation*. Griffith and his brother, R. E., invested their own money in filmmaking in New Mexico by building a hotel in Gallup (see location 39). The El Rancho Hotel, they reasoned, would be a convenient staging area for Western producers who wanted to capture the scenic region on film.

OUTDOOR RECREATION

In the winter, Ski Santa Fe (see location 11) offers a good mix of novice and expert runs. In the summer, nearby trails offer incredible views and relief from the heat. The same can be said of the Sandia Mountains (see location 27) bordering Albuquerque. Both provide mountainous scenery in easy driving distance.

Los Alamos (see location 14), best known as the home of the Manhattan Project during World War II, is also surrounded by verdant peaks that are great for hiking. There are trails throughout the Valles Caldera (see location 15) and in the surrounding Jemez Mountains, which will look familiar to fans of the television show *Longmire*.

Kirk Douglas with the Sandia Mountains in the background in *Lonely are the Brave* (1962). Courtesy of the Paul Andrew Hutton Collection and Universal Pictures.

PART II

SANTA FE AREA

Arnold Schwarzenegger and Danny DeVito in front of the Cathedral Basilica of St. Francis of Assisi in *Twins* (1988). Courtesy of Universal Pictures.

1

SANTA FE PLAZA AND DOWNTOWN SANTA FE

The heart of New Mexico is also at the center of many films and television shows.

Officially the second capital of Spanish New Mexico, Santa Fe was founded in 1610 by Don Pedro de Peralta. The Spanish colonists built a secure plaza and fort that soon became the center of local activity. The colonists also built a seat for their officials, which they called the Palace of the Governors (105 West Palace Ave, Santa Fe, NM, 87501; 505-476-5100, nmhistorymuseum.org). The building is still standing and is now a museum administered by the State of New Mexico. The Palace is attached to the New Mexico History Museum (113 Lincoln Ave, Santa Fe, NM, 87501; 505-476-5200, nmhistory museum.org), which features information on the state's past.

In 1821, Santa Fe, along with the rest of Nueva España, passed into Mexican control. Soon thereafter, the city became the terminus of the Santa Fe Trail and an important trading hub in the Southwest. The Trail itself stretched eight hundred miles from Santa Fe to Independence, Missouri, where it met up with a variety of other land and water routes. Manufactured goods flowed west, and furs flowed east. The Trail was short-lived, however, and all but ended when the United States took control of New Mexico in 1848. The Plaza and activity around the Palace of Governors began to shrink as permanent Territorial-era buildings were constructed on all sides.

Santa Fe quieted until the railroad arrived in 1880 and brought with it waves of tourists. Visitors craved an exotic Southwest flavor, and over the next few decades many buildings adopted a Spanish and Pueblo Revival style of architecture, cementing the look of the "City Different," as Santa Fe has come to be called, in adobe mud.

Now one of the oldest cities in North America, Santa Fe is the crown jewel of New Mexico. It's the epicenter of tourism in the state and home to a surprising number of museums. The Georgia O'Keeffe Museum (217 Johnson Street, Santa Fe, NM, 87501; 505-946-1000, okeeffemuseum.org) celebrates the painter and made a brief appearance in *Breaking Bad*. The New Mexico Museum of Art (107 West Palace Avenue, Santa Fe, NM, 87501; 505-476-5072, nmartmuseum.org) has a collection that focuses on art from the state. Off the Plaza, Museum Hill (710 Camino Lejo off Old Santa Fe Trail, Santa Fe, NM, 87505; 505-476-1269, museumhill.net) is a collection of museums gathered around a sculpture garden.

Santa Fe Plaza itself, once an alfalfa farm, is now a carefully maintained park, often filled with musicians and Native American artists selling their wares. Several major events draw tens of thousands of people to the Plaza each year. The Southwestern Association for Indian Arts organizes the annual Santa Fe Indian Market (swaia.org) every August. The event is the largest of its kind in the world. Every autumn, the Plaza hosts the Fiestas de Santa Fe. Once a celebration of the Spanish Reconquest, the weekend-long party now is best known for honoring reinvention by destroying a massive marionette of Old Man Gloom, a.k.a. the Zozobra (burnzozobra.com). This physical embodiment of the previous year's "anguish, anxiety, and gloom" is set ablaze in front of a raucous crowd just off the Plaza on the Friday before Labor Day.

The Fiestas were the backdrop for a noir mystery in *Ride the*

Pink Horse. Directed by and starring Robert Montgomery, the film follows a recently returned World War II veteran who goes to the fictional town of San Pablo, New Mexico, to blackmail a crime boss. Much of the flick revolves around Montgomery's failure to understand New Mexico traditions. Zozobra makes a starring appearance.

The landmark road-trip movie *Powwow Highway*, based on the novel of the same name by David Seals, was shot on the Plaza in 1988. Directed by Jonathan Wacks and starring A. Martinez and Gary Farmer, the film features two Native American men who cross the country to rescue one of their sisters. Actors Graham Greene and Wes Studi, who would both go on to prominent careers, had small parts in the movie. After filming, Wacks, Farmer, and Studi all moved to Santa Fe.

With a view of the Plaza and a full menu of New Mexican classics, the Plaza Café (54 Lincoln Avenue, Santa Fe, NM, 87501; 505-982-1664, plazacafesantafe.com) appeared in *Did You Hear About the Morgans?* The witness-protection comedy starred Hugh Grant and Sarah Jessica Parker as a troubled couple who see a murder and then have to go into hiding. The Plaza Café also popped up in the television series *Graves*. The show featured Nick Nolte as a former president of the United States who comes to regret the policies he enacted while in office. Instead of enjoying his retirement, Nolte attempts to undo some of the damage he did while in office. He goes to the Plaza Café to talk to real people.

Only a block away from the Plaza stands the Cathedral Basilica of Saint Francis de Assisi (131 Cathedral Place, Santa Fe, NM, 87501; 505-982-5619, cbsfa.org). Completed in 1886, the Saint Francis Cathedral is an architectural gem. Commissioned by Archbishop Jean Baptiste Lamy, who would later be the subject of the Willa Cather novel *Death Comes for the Archbishop*, the cathedral is Romanesque Revival in style and made of stone instead of adobe. European masons working in New Mexico were responsible for the elaborate carvings.

The cathedral fills a few of the frames in the quirky comedy

ALTITUDE

At almost seven thousand feet in elevation, Santa Fe is well over a mile above sea level, and people from lower elevations will likely feel the effects. The easiest way to avoid altitude sickness or exhaustion is to drink lots of water and stay hydrated. On hot days, this is especially important.

Twins, which stars Arnold Schwarzenegger and Danny DeVito. Directed by Ivan Reitman of *Ghostbusters* fame, the film follows Schwarzenegger as he searches for lost family. Turns out that both Schwarzenegger and DeVito were created by genetic engineering, but DeVito was the refuse of the project. The two twins travel all over the Southwest in search of their mother.

Not far from the cathedral, the adobe Loretto Chapel (207 Old Santa Fe Trail, Santa Fe, NM, 87501; 505-982-0092, lorettochapel .com) is famed for its miraculous staircase. According to lore, a mysterious woodworker arrived at the chapel in the late nineteenth century in answer to the prayers of nuns at the chapel. That woodworker built a spiral staircase to second-story seating without support and using no nails. The staircase appears to float in the back of the chapel. This architectural oddity was the subject of a 1988 television film starring William Peterson and Barbara Hershey. *The Staircase* was filmed in Santa Fe. The USA Network procedural series *In Plain Sight*, which based productions in Albuquerque, later used the chapel for an episode segment set in England, because of its period look.

The flamboyantly pink Santa Fe Scottish Rite Center, just a few blocks away, was featured in the series *Perpetual Grace, LTD* and decorated as an English orphanage in which Sir Ben Kingsley's character spent time as a youth. The film *Finch*, starring Tom Hanks, features the fanciful theater on the interior. The building is located on the corner of Bishop's Lodge Road and Paseo de Peralta.

CREW MEMORY

If you want publicity for your show, film it on the Santa Fe Plaza. The hub of this art town of seventy thousand, the Plaza is always high-visibility. When we were filming *Graves* at the Plaza Café, word got out fast! We attracted impromptu visits first from a Santa Fe New Mexican photographer, then a reporter from that newspaper, and then the mayor. The next day, a big photo of Nick Nolte resting on a bench outside the restaurant was splashed across page one of the papers. Our show also made use of the very colorful holiday lights that go up on the Plaza on Thanksgiving weekend and remain up for months. —*Wolf Schneider, Unit Publicist*

HOW TO GET THERE

The Santa Fe Plaza is at the corner of Old Santa Fe Trail and West Palace Avenue. Santa Fe is served by Interstate 25 and a municipal airport.

WHERE TO STAY

Inn of the Five Graces
150 East De Vargas Street
Santa Fe, NM 87501
505-992-0957
fivegraces.com

This Middle Eastern–themed hotel is a posh selection for productions with deep pockets.

WHERE TO EAT

Rio Chama Prime Steakhouse
414 Old Santa Fe Trail
Santa Fe, NM 87501
505-955-0765
riochamasantafe.com

During the legislative session every year, state delegates fill the booths at this sprawling, ambiance-filled steak joint. The occasional production team will stop in for meetings as well.

SELECTED FILMOGRAPHY

Montgomery, Robert, dir. *Ride the Pink Horse*. USA: Universal Pictures, 1947. Film.

Reitman, Ivan, dir. *Twins*. USA: Universal Pictures, 1988. Film.

Wacks, Jonathan, dir. *Powwow Highway*. USA: Warner Bros., 1989. Film.

Arthur, Karen, dir. *The Staircase*. USA: CBS, 1998. TV movie.

Lawrence, Marc, dir. *Did You Hear About the Morgans?* USA: Columbia Pictures, 2009. Film.

Conrad, Steve, and Bruce Terris, creators. *Perpetual Grace, LTD.* USA: MGM Television, 2019–. Television series.

Sapochnik, Miguel, dir. *Finch*. USA: Universal Pictures, 2021. Film.

2

SANTA FE LIKE A FILM LOCAL

Santa Fe is home to a host of well-known filmmakers. They were all, with little doubt, drawn by Santa Fe's artistic heritage, which began thousands of years ago but gelled into its modern form under the influence of the Museum of New Mexico. The museum promoted New Mexico's Puebloan traditions and arts. A decade later, artist's colonies opened in Santa Fe and Taos, establishing the out-of-the way capital as a destination for creative personalities. It helped that a series of national magazines proclaimed the City Different as a top place to live in the 1980s.

As the population grew, so did the gallery scene. The city is now home to hundreds of galleries that represent artists in almost every medium. Galleries are scattered throughout the city, but many are concentrated on Canyon Road.

A recent addition to the museum and art scene, Meow Wolf's House of Eternal Return (1352 Rufina Circle, Santa Fe, NM, 87507; 505-395-6369, meowwolf.com) has rapidly gained a huge following. The mixed-use, mixed-media space combines narrative and technology in a cavernous recycled bowling alley. Created by the Meow Wolf Artists' collaborative, the House of Eternal Return is an interactive art installation that is part Disneyland, part haunted house, and part jungle gym, all done up in neon colors and glow-in-the-dark paints. The interactive space is a must-see. Also be on the lookout for the schedule of concerts and art classes for adults and children. The collaborative hosts parties and events in both Santa Fe and Taos. It's also expanded to locations in Denver, Colorado, and Las Vegas, Nevada.

Santa Fe is also a magnet for the culinary arts. Many of the restaurants in Santa Fe concentrate around the historic plaza. The Coyote Cafe & Cantina (132 West Water Street, Santa Fe, NM,

Lobby card for *Ride the Pink Horse* (1947). Courtesy of the Paul Andrew Hutton Collection and Universal Pictures.

87501; 505-983-1615, coyotecafe.com) is a classic choice for upscale Southwestern Cuisine. The attached Coyote Cantina on the Rooftop has great views and some creative drink offerings. Billing itself as "Santa Fe's Watering Hole" and drawing a consistent stream of locals, nearby Del Charro (101 West Alameda Street, Santa Fe, NM, 87501; 505-954-0320, delcharro.com) offers reasonably priced margaritas and hamburgers.

Canyon Road also has several outstanding, but expensive, fine-dining establishments. Geronimo (724 Canyon Road, Santa Fe, NM, 87501; 505-982-1500, geronimorestaurant.com) may be the most acclaimed restaurant in town and is a magnet for visiting film directors and producers. They serve "global eclectic" cuisine. Across the street, The Compound (653 Canyon Road A, Santa Fe, NM, 87501; 505-982-4353, compoundrestaurant.com) is another good choice for award-winning food in an intimate historic building. Try El Farol (808 Canyon Road, Santa Fe, NM, 87501; 505-983-9912, elfarolsantafe.com) for tapas, live music, and flamenco dancing.

Warren Oates, Dennis Wilson, and James Taylor in *Two-Lane Blacktop* (1971).
Courtesy of the Paul Andrew Hutton Collection and Universal Pictures.

Other drinking and popular late-night options include Tonic (103 East Water Street, Santa Fe, NM, 87501; 505-982-1189, tonic santafe.com), which serves mixed drinks and panache in a faux speakeasy setting. Boxcar (530 South Guadalupe Street, Santa Fe, NM, 87501; 505-988-7222, boxcarsantafe.com) at the Railyard is the best spot for watching sports on television.

Like Albuquerque, Santa Fe is home to a bevy of microbreweries. Some are, in fact, not so micro. Santa Fe Brewing Company claims it was the earliest of the local beer operations and is now one of the largest beer makers in the state. Their flagship venue and beer hall (35 Fire Place, Santa Fe, NM, 87508; 505-424-3333, santafebrewing.com) has a concert stage. Second Street Brewery has a location at its namesake and another at the Railyard (1607 Paseo De Peralta, Santa Fe, NM, 87501; 505-989-3278, secondstreet brewery.com).

For live theater and lectures, the Lensic Performing Arts Center (211 West San Francisco Street, Santa Fe, NM, 8750; 505-988-1234, lensic.org) is a premier destination. Author George R. R. Martin invested some of his Game of Thrones mega-fame into ownership of the Jean Cocteau Theater and its attached bookstore (418 Montezuma Avenue, Santa Fe, NM, 87501; 505-466-5528, jeancocteau cinema.com). The Cocteau screens quirky and cult films and hosts local film events. A few blocks away, the Violet Crown (1606 Alcaldesa St, Santa Fe, NM, 87501; 505-216-5678, santafe.violetcrown .com) serves beer and food with their showings.

Santa Fe is surrounded by opportunities for outdoor recreation as well. Hyde Park Road starts near the plaza and eventually moves up to Ski Santa Fe (see location 11). The Dale Ball Trail (sfct. org/dale-ball-trails) system, only a few miles up the mountain from Santa Fe, has a selection of trails that are great for both walking and mountain biking. Nearby Hyde Memorial State Park (740 Hyde Park Road, Santa Fe, NM, 87501; 505-983-7175, emnrd. state.nm.us/SPD/hydememorialstatepark.html) bills itself as New Mexico's first state park. It features a selection of trails as well as camping spots.

3

OLD MAIN STATE PENITENTIARY

Once the site of a gruesome prison revolt, this disused state penitentiary was partially remodeled for the remake of The Longest Yard *(2005).*

Built in 1956 to hold prisoners for the entire state, the Old Main quickly grew overcrowded. In 1980 inmates rioted and took over the facility. After taking possession of the control tower, the prisoners effectively had complete charge of the Old Main. Twelve officers were taken hostage while inmates raped, mutilated, and tortured each other. Altogether, thirty-three people were killed before prisoners surrendered to the National Guard. Despite the nightmarish violence, the Old Main reopened and was in use until 1998. That year, a newer penitentiary opened across the street and currently serves the State of New Mexico.

The penitentiary returned to life almost immediately as a film set and separately as a training ground for the Department of Corrections. In 2003, the Adam Sandler film *The Longest Yard* used the Old Main to stand in for a fictional correctional facility in Allenville, Texas. In a remake of the Burt Reynolds film of the same name, a group of prisoners prepares for and plays the prison guards in an overly aggressive game of football.

To transform the Old Main, the production built two football fields with bleachers, a few ancillary buildings, two towers, and a new frontage for one of the old cell blocks. All told, the additions cost about $4 million dollars, and some of them are still visible from the exterior of the prison on the southernmost cell block

If the set had an air of authenticity, the cast did as well. To complement star Adam Sandler, former professional football players,

The Old Main State Penitentiary as it appears in *The Longest Yard* (2005). Courtesy of Paramount Pictures.

Nikolaj Coster-Waldau in front of the Old Main State Penitentiary in *Shot Caller* (2017). Courtesy of Relativity Media.

pro wrestlers, and body builders were hired to play both cons and prison guards. For the climactic game, the *x*'s and *o*'s were drawn up by National Football League coach Jon Gruden and Arena Football League quarterback / offensive coordinator Pat O'Hara. When not playing and coaching, O'Hara acted in or advised on almost a dozen films featuring football, including *The Waterboy*, Sandler's previous football flick.

The Longest Yard set a precedent at the Old Main. At least a dozen films followed, taking advantage of the building's interior cells and shops. Director Ric Roman Waugh made two films about prison life using the Old Main. The first, *Felon*, is based on violent episodes at a prison in California and follows an everyday man as he adjusts to life on the inside. Stephen Dorff starred in the film as a convicted killer. A decade later he returned to New Mexico to play a sheriff in the Fox television show *Deputy*. Waugh's second film is about internal prison politics and featured *Game of Thrones* star Nicolaj Coster-Waldau as the proverbial *Shot Caller*.

Initially, the Old Main offered only occasional tours. Popular demand increased, though, and now regular tours are scheduled on the first two Saturdays of all

HOW TO GET THERE

4311 New Mexico State Road 14
Santa Fe, NM 87502
cd.nm.gov/old-main

No one will be admitted to the Old Main while carrying a firearm, and no children under the age of sixteen are allowed.

WHERE TO STAY

La Posada de Santa Fe
330 East Palace Avenue
Santa Fe, NM 87501
505-986-0000
laposadadesantafe.com

WHERE TO EAT

Beer Creek Brewing Co.
3810 State Road 14
Santa Fe, NM 87508
505-471-9271
beercreekbrew.com

summer months. Tickets must be reserved in advance. Run by the New Mexico Corrections Department, these guided walk-throughs are based strictly on evidentiary records.

SELECTED FILMOGRAPHY

Segal, Peter, dir. *The Longest Yard*. USA: Paramount Pictures, 2005. Film.

Waugh, Ric Roman, dir. *Felon*. USA: Sony Pictures, 2008. Film.

———. *Shot Caller*. USA: Saban Films, 2017. Film.

4

EL RANCHO DE LAS GOLONDRINAS

This model pioneer village south of Santa Fe makes a convenient period backdrop for Westerns like The Kid.

In a send-up of the 1980s television hit *MacGyver*, comedian Will Forte stars as a bumbling intelligence agent named MacGruber. Unlike the television MacGyver, the facsimile MacGruber does not have the skills to escape death traps with hastily assembled gadgets. Instead, he relies on his training and an incredibly blunt attitude. On occasion, he saves himself with a piece of celery protruding from an unsavory orifice.

After a tragedy, MacGruber resets himself at an isolated monastery high in the mountains, and that's where the self-titled, cult comedy film starts. Of course, the monastery used in the film is not in isolated mountains, but just miles from Santa Fe at El Rancho de las Golondrinas (the Ranch of the Swallows).

Now an interactive museum, Las Golondrinas was once a working ranch along El Camino Real Tierra Adentro (Royal Road of the Interior).The road ran from Mexico City to just north of Santa Fe and was an essential commercial corridor that moved goods throughout Nueva España. El Rancho de Las Golondrinas was one of a number of residences built along the old route as an official rest stop for travelers.

In addition to housing travelers, Las Golondrinas functioned as a true working ranch starting in the 1700s. A nearby running stream gave farmers an opportunity to build acequias (small canals) and divert water to their crops in an otherwise dry landscape. Later, the ranch added a trading post to its repertoire.

In the 1960s, the owner of the historic rancho transformed it into a living-history museum by relocating a number of antique buildings onto the property. The property now has more than

Ethan Hawke, playing Sheriff Pat Garrett in *The Kid* (2019), arrives at El Rancho de las Golondrinas. Courtesy of Lionsgate.

thirty-three buildings from almost every era of New Mexico history.

These antique buildings make Las Golondrinas the perfect location for period films. Numerous Westerns have used the rancho, beginning with the sequel to *Butch Cassidy and the Sundance Kid*. The smash hit, which challenged traditional Westerns and cemented Robert Redford as an international star, didn't leave much room for a follow-up film (because they died at the end). Academy Award–winning writer William Goldman had an idea, though. He suggested to a producer that they make a film that focused on the rise of the young outlaws.

Goldman declined to work on the film, and so did stars Redford and Paul Newman. Instead, the production selected Tom Berenger to play Butch Cassidy and William Katt as the Sundance Kid. Both looked similar enough to their predecessors to play them in *Butch and Sundance: The Early Days*. The production shot throughout New Mexico and Southern Colorado. At Las Golondrinas, the film built a nineteenth-century mining office, which is still standing. The building was the first addition to Las Golondrinas made by a film and has been featured in a number of subsequent movies and televisions shows.

Over thirty films in almost every genre followed in the footsteps of *Butch and Sundance: The Early Days* at Las Golondrinas. The general manager of the property, John Berkenfield, told the *Albuquerque Journal* a story about the making of a romantic comedy called *Fools Rush In*, which featured Salma Hayek as a Mexican national who falls in love with an American who is unprepared for their cultural differences. Las Golondrinas subbed in for Hayek's village in Mexico. "There's a scene when Salma is taking a swim in a lake," he says. "In the movie it looks like it's a hundred degrees. In reality, it was forty degrees, and the director kept stopping the scene because she was getting goosebumps." She would get out of the water, and the crew would immediately put blankets on her, Geary explains. "As soon as she got warm, it was back into the water."

Las Golondrinas also subbed in for Southern New Mexico. In *The Kid*, Las Golondrinas acts as Pete Maxwell's house, where Billy the Kid famously met his end, asking, "Quien es?" quietly to the darkness. The real Maxwell House where Billy the Kid met his end at the hands of Sheriff Pat Garrett is closer to Fort Sumner.

Based on the novel of the same name by Paulette Jiles, *News of the World* also made use of Las Golondrinas. Directed by Paul Greengrass, the film stars Tom Hanks as a Texan traveling across the West and reading the news to local townspeople. His uncom-

HOW TO GET THERE

334 Los Pinos Road
Santa Fe, NM 87507
505-471-2261
golondrinas.org

Open dates and hours are subject to change.

WHERE TO STAY

Hotel Chimayó de Santa Fe
125 Washington Avenue
Santa Fe, NM 87501
505-988-4900
hotelchimayo.com

WHERE TO EAT

Shake Foundation
631 Cerrillos Road
Santa Fe, NM 87501
505-988-8992
shakefoundation.com

And its sister restaurant:

Taco Fundacíon
235 North Guadalupe
Santa Fe, NM 87501
505-982-8286

Although Shake Foundation serves the burgers, Taco Fundacíon operates out of a historic burger shack. For years, Bert's Burger Bowl was a popular hangout for Santa Feans and played a big role in the road-trip flick *Two-Lane Blacktop*. Director Monte Hellman called the place a "real popular teen hangout." Singer James Taylor, in the lead role, goes to Bert's Burger Bowl to challenge an unsuspecting local to a race. Taylor wins the race easily and puts the local, played by the film's screenwriter, to shame.

plicated mission changes when he agrees to help recover a kidnapped girl.

Las Golondrinas is only open during the spring for docent-led tours. Over the summer, self-guided tours are available. The rancho hosts a number of special events, including a Renaissance Faire, a wine festival, and a beer festival. During some special occasions, Las Golondrinas features living-history demonstrations.

For the full pampering experience after an event, try nearby Sunrise Springs Spa Resort for a soak and a massage. The sister property of Ojo Caliente (242 Los Pinos Road, Santa Fe, NM, 87507; 877-977-8212, ojosantafe.ojospa.com) features guest rooms and pools.

SELECTED FILMOGRAPHY

Lester, Richard, dir. *Butch & Sundance: The Early Days*. USA: Twentieth Century Fox, 1979. Film.
Tennant, Andy, dir. *Fools Rush In*. USA: Columbia Pictures, 1997. Film.
Taccone, Jorma, dir. *MacGruber*. USA: Lionsgate, 2010. Film.
D'Onofrio, Vincent, dir. *The Kid*. USA: Lionsgate, 2019. Film.

Bonanza Creek Ranch (2017). Photo by Celli Crawford.

5

BONANZA CREEK RANCH

Since 1955, this working ranch has hosted dozens of films.

Before Bonanza Creek Ranch became the home for the faux American West, it was home to the real Western tradition. In 1879, a small mineral strike led to the creation of a short-lived boomtown named Bonanza City. At its peak the city was home to several hundred people and a smelter for processing metals. The mines didn't last long, and Bonanza City was all but gone by 1884. The area, though, has a fairly steady supply of water and became an active cattle ranch, and it stayed that way until Jimmy Stewart arrived in 1954.

Legend has it that an old friend of silent-film star Mary Pickford moved to Albuquerque looking for a new start but kept his Hollywood contacts and brought friends out to New Mexico to show off some possible filming locations. The Jarrett Ranch (as it was known then) possessed stark mountain views, and no modern structures were in sight. It was ideal for a Western, and it became the site of the final collaboration between actor Jimmy Stewart and director Anthony Mann.

Mann got his start in the theater and moved on to direct noir films in the 1940s. He found critical and commercial success with a slew of Westerns including *The Furies* and *Winchester '73*, both released in 1950. Stewart starred in *Winchester '73* and then worked with Mann on seven subsequent films. Mann eventually garnered a reputation for making dark, genre-bending Westerns. Stewart's work with Mann allowed him to play more grim parts than were previously allowed by his reputation as a wholesome actor.

For *The Man from Laramie*, Mann drew inspiration from Shakespeare's *King Lear* to tell the story of an aggrieved cowboy who finds himself caught in the crosshairs of an evil, New Mexico cattle baron. The Jarrett Ranch stood in for the fictional ranch in the film.

Cowboy, starring Glenn Ford and Jack Lemmon, followed *The Man from Laramie*, establishing Jarrett Ranch as a preeminent Western destination. Over the next few decades, a number of other productions took advantage of the clean skylines of the ranch. Some made slight additions to the ranch and built parts of sets, like barns and false fronts. The owners of the ranch attempted to keep up the sets built for *The Legend of the Lone Ranger* in the late 1970s, but they proved too flimsy. "It was all false fronts, and we had a horrible time with it, with walls always blowing over. So we tore it down," said owner Glenn Hughes, who had hoped to preserve them for future use.

An Italian television show called *Lucky Luke* changed the face of the ranch in the late 1980s. *Lucky Luke*, directed by and starring Terence Hill, added a stylized and expansive period town. The production built some twenty-five structures in a flat space, not far from the three distinctive hills that mark the landscape. *Lucky Luke* only ran for a pilot feature and one season, but Hill returned to the ranch with another film. For *Botte di Natale* (Christmas Fight) Hill's team built a home by the pond on Bonanza Creek, on the other side of the ranch. Both the home set and the town became staples of Westerns filming in New Mexico. The "Pond House," as it came to be called, appeared in *Perpetual Grace, LTD* as the home of Sir Ben Kingsley's character.

Bonanza Creek Ranch (2016). Photo by Celli Crawford.

Bonanza Creek has been used for non-Westerns as well. Billy Bob Thornton, for instance, launched a homemade spaceship from a barn built just feet away from Hill's Pond House in *The Astronaut Farmer*. This was something of a sci-fi film, in which Thornton plays a former Air Force officer with dreams of exploration that pit him against the government and the establishment.

More in the genre of science fact than science fiction, the short-lived television show *Manhattan*, about the invention of the atomic bomb, built World War II–era homes near the site of the old ghost town and used them for several seasons. After the show was canceled, the ranch left the faux prefabs in place. Savvy producers on the Christian Bale Western *Hostiles* asked for permission to move the structures and reposition them as part of a late nineteenth-century fort. The *Hostiles* crew built another fort just up the road for the opening sequence of the film. The massive set proved so dusty that the shoot had to pause on occasion to allow the clouds to settle.

More recently, the Disney+ movie *Stargirl*, based on the popular Jerry Spinelli teen novel, used a remote cabin at Bonanza Creek as the home of a scientist played by Giancarlo Esposito of *Breaking Bad* fame.

One of the busiest filming locations in New Mexico, Bonanza Creek Ranch is also open for tours and private events.

CREW MEMORY

I remember one day shooting a pilot for one of the big online streaming services in Ford's Ranch in the Galisteo Basin. It was a blistering day, and by midday most of the crew looked like ghosts—pale, sweaty apparitions of their former selves. But by late afternoon dark clouds had rolled in, and a heavy quiet seemed to settle on everything. No one really knows that New Mexico has a monsoon season—actual rain falls from the actual sky. Sometimes in a way that seems eerily Biblical. The Hollywood set are always amazed.

Things got Biblical in a hurry. What started as a lightning delay turned in into an all-out evacuation after about ten minutes. Everything that once resembled a road turned into a mud pit. The main street, down the center of town, turned into a river. Crew members scrambled desperately to get camera and lighting equipment to shelter. The transpo vans were sliding all over the roads and started getting stuck. Cast members were marooned in the old leaky buildings. Tony Mark, the production manager got his personal vehicle—an old Ford Bronco—and started transporting members of the cast back to basecamp. It took hours to get everybody out. Transpo had use of a Pettibone—a massive piece of machinery that resembles a giant crab—to pull the vans out of the muck. I pushed cars out of the mud with the locations crew for hours after wrap. It was a glorious disaster. I've never worked on

OTHER FILM RANCHES

Film crews will shoot in real locations, but controlled environments are far easier to manipulate and often preferable. When possible, productions or studios build and then reuse "backlots" or facsimile towns that they own and can change at will. Especially with period pieces, it's simpler for shooting crews to use backlots or ranches that are devoid of modern trappings that must be obscured or removed.

New Mexico is home to several film ranches and backlots, all of which are tailor made for Westerns. In addition to the Bonanza and J. W. Eaves Movie Ranches (see location 6), the other frequently used movie ranch in New Mexico was called the Cook Ranch (or the Ford Ranch when owned by fashion icon Tom Ford) and is now known as the Cerro Pelon Ranch and is not typically open to the public. Screenwriter and director Lawrence Kasdan, famed for his work on *Indiana Jones and the Raiders of the Lost Ark*, brought his underappreciated Western *Silverado* to the ranch in 1985. They built a small town to accommodate the shoot. Later, that same town appeared as a modern hamlet in Marvel Studios' *Thor* and is prominently visible in the battle between the title hero and a metallic monster sent to earth to destroy him. (Prefiguring *Thor* in the Marvel Studios series, *Iron Man 2* makes mention of New Mexico. Robert Downey Jr. as Tony Stark cracks a "Land of Enchantment" joke.) The film site is part of a massive, private ranch that includes a tennis court and pool.

The Netflix Western miniseries *Godless* was shot at Bonanza Creek Ranch and the Cerro Pelon Ranch, but it also constructed its own town at the San Cristobal Ranch, south of Lamy. The series is about a mining town in which all the men died in a mining accident and the women take control of the area. The show was written and directed by film veteran Scott Frank who followed it up with the highly successful show *The Queen's Gambit.*

San Cristobal also played a prevalent role in the Coen Brothers' *True Grit*. The cast and crew were on sight so frequently that actor Jeff Bridges commissioned a helicopter landing pad for his commute.

HOW TO GET THERE

From I-25, take Entrada La Cienega, exit 271, then head south on the frontage road to Bonanza Creek Road. Turn left at the dirt road after about one mile. A small guard shack marks the turnoff.

15 Bonanza Creek Lane
Santa Fe, NM 87508
505-471-4248
bonanzacreekranch.com

Please check ahead for tour times and availability.

WHERE TO STAY

Drury Plaza Hotel in Santa Fe
828 Paseo de Peralta
Santa Fe, NM 87501
505-424-2175
druryhotels.com/locations/santa-fe-nm/drury-plaza-hotel-in-santa-fe

Designed by architect John Gaw Meem, the building that is now the Drury Hotel began its life as the St. Vincent's Hospital in the 1950s. Built at the request of the Sisters of Charity, who had previously run a care facility affiliated with the Cathedral Basilica, St. Vincent's operated in this Plaza location until 1977. The building, a sterling example of Territorial Revival design, then housed the New Mexico Department of Cultural Affairs and the New Mexico Film Commission. A number of films and television shows also used the vacant hospital. It was featured in the Judy Blume adaptation *Tiger Eyes* and in Marvel Studios' *Thor*. The hotel is popular with productions.

WHERE TO EAT

Jambo Café
2010 Cerrillos Road
Santa Fe, NM 87505
505-473-1269
jambocafe.net

This Caribbean and African food restaurant in southern Santa Fe is a hit among crew members. Make sure to try the curry dipping sauce.

a set where the monsoon season didn't cost at least a day of work on location to get canceled. New Mexico always seems to exact its special share of the fun. —*Kirt Bozeman, Screenwriter*

CREW MEMORY

Man, does the Ford Ranch get dark at night. One night we were doing an electronic press kit interview on *Appaloosa* after company wrap. When we finished, Transpo whisked the talent away. Everyone else had wrapped, and there were no lights on anywhere. I wandered around in the pitch blackness looking for where I'd parked my car and trying not to panic. Luckily, one last crew member drove through to make sure everyone had left, and I flagged them down! —*Wolf Schneider, Unit Publicist*

SELECTED FILMOGRAPHY

Branagh, Kenneth, dir. *Thor*. USA: Marvel Studios, 2011. Film.

Favreau, Jon, dir. *Cowboys & Aliens*. USA: Universal Pictures, 2011. Film.

Frank, Scott, dir. *Godless*. USA: Netflix, 2017. TV mini-series.

Hill, Terence, dir. *Lucky Luke*. USA: A-Pix Entertainment, 2000. DVD.

———. *Botte di Natale*. Italy: Rialto Films, 1994. Film.

Kasdan, Lawrence, dir. *Silverado*. USA: Columbia Pictures, 1985. Film.

———. *Wyatt Earp*. USA: Warner Bros., 1994. Film.

Kelly, Gene, dir. *The Cheyenne Social Club*. USA: National General Productions, 1970. Film.

Mann, Anthony, dir. *The Man from Laramie*. USA: Columbia Pictures, 1955. Film.

Polish, Michael, dir. *The Astronaut Farmer*. USA: Warner Bros., 2006. Film.

The J. W. Eaves Movie Ranch (2012). Photo by Celli Crawford.

6

J. W. EAVES MOVIE RANCH

Eaves was instrumental in the creation of the modern New Mexico film business.

Jesse Willard Eaves was born in Texas in 1916 and spent some time in the local oil fields before he moved to Illinois. There, he found his way into the trucking business. Willard did well in the trucking world and eventually took ownership of an outfit that grew into a fleet of over 150 trucks. Looking to diversify, Eaves and his family purchased a tract of land south of Santa Fe called Rancho Allegre. They filled the property with cattle.

While Eaves was tending the herd one day, a producer walked up to him and asked if he could use the area as the backdrop for a Western television show called *Empire*. At first, Eaves didn't believe the man, but when his incredulity passed, Eaves realized this was potentially a significant source of income. He could rent the ranch out for Western productions and still maintain his cattle and horses.

Empire, created by one of the writers of the television show *Bonanza*, only ran for one and a half seasons on NBC. The show had tremendous star power, however. It featured Ryan O'Neal

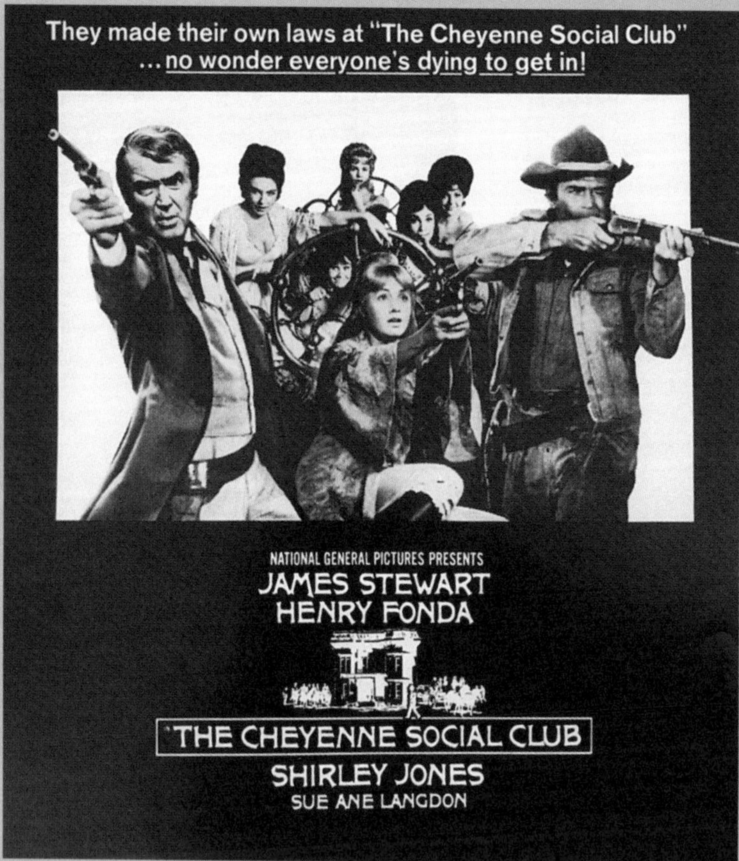

Ad for *The Cheyenne Social Club* (1970). Courtesy of the Paul Andrew Hutton Collection and National General Productions.

and Charles Bronson, who both went on to major film careers. *Empire* also shot around Santa Fe and Española.

After *Empire*, the ranch found its way into the Hollywood rotation. A pair of comedies about students at a religious school filmed at Eaves Ranch in the late 1960s. *The Trouble With Angels* and *Where Angels Go, Trouble Follows* both featured Rosalind Russell as a mother superior tending to troublesome girls.

Meanwhile, author Max Evans and an assortment of New Mexico film-industry promoters began their push for Hollywood producers to bring shows to New Mexico. The group soon found that they needed a standing Western town setting to truly attract productions. Eaves was game for the arrangement. Evans and his team worked with the production designer of the *Angels* films to get some ideas for a permanent backlot. In 1968, plans were made, and the town site was feted. Evans, as he suspected, had little trouble getting studio heads to commit to shooting in New Mexico with the Western lot as bait.

The Cheyenne Social Club was the first film to pay a visit to the newly completed backlot at Eaves Ranch in 1969. The comedy starred Jimmy Stewart as a cowboy who inherits possession of a

HOW TO GET THERE

75 Rancho Alegre Road
Santa Fe, NM 87508
505-474-3045

WHERE TO STAY

El Rey Court
1862 Cerrillos Road
Santa Fe, NM 87505
505-982-1931
elreycourt.com

The El Rey Court was recently rehabbed, and its attached bar, La Reina, is a popular hangout.

WHERE TO EAT

San Marcos Café & Feed Store
3877 New Mexico State Road 14
Santa Fe, NM 87508
505-471-9298

Richard Egan and Terry Moore in *Empire* (1962–1964). Courtesy of the Paul Andrew Hutton Collection and NBC.

brothel. Gene Kelly, the famed dancer and actor, directed the film. The film, and the Western town, cemented Eaves Ranch as a popular destination, consistently drawing productions in the years that followed.

Over its long history, the ranch has also been opened to the community for events and festivals. It hosted the Thirsty Ears Festival for a decade. The gathering featured roots rock, bluegrass, and country bands from all over the country. Public tours were not available when this book was published.

SELECTED FILMOGRAPHY

Hite, Kathleen, dir. *Empire*. USA: NBC, 1962–1964. TV series.

Kelly, Gene, dir. *The Cheyenne Social Club*. USA: National General Pictures, 1970. Film.

Lupino, Ida, dir. *The Trouble with Angels*. USA: Columbia Pictures, 1966. Film.

———. *Where Angels Go, Trouble Follows*. USA: Columbia Pictures, 1968. Film.

7

CERRILLOS

This old mining town later boomed with Westerns.

It won't take much imagination to picture Cerrillos as a Western town. The former mining village has barely changed over the last century.

Turquoise mines near Cerrillos first opened sometime around CE 900. The Pueblo people who retrieved the semiprecious stone traded it throughout the Southwest. Over the centuries, other mines in the area produced silver, galena, lead, and gold. Investments in the mines expanded in the 1870s and brought a frenzy of miners and attendant businesses. When the railroad arrived in 1880, Cerrillos truly boomed. The town had saloons, a Wells Fargo branch, and even a hotel.

That boomtown look brought Hollywood calling in the 1950s with, of all things, a true New Mexico story. Following the smash success of their *Davy Crockett* series, Disney programmed additional Western series. One of these shows starred Robert Loggia as a real-life frontier hero named Elfego Baca. Born in Socorro in 1865, Baca became a lawman at just nineteen years of age. He developed a reputation for being a good shot and for being all but impossible to kill. Baca survived multiple attempts on his life and went on to become a lawyer and politician. The larger-than-life Baca proved to be just about the right size for Disney, with Loggia as the Hispanic lawman.

Despite his impressive career, Baca's fame pales in comparison to that of Billy the Kid (see location 40). The teenage killer outgrew his short life to become an international celebrity. It's therefore fitting that the film *Young Guns* features a cast of a handful

Cerrillos as it appeared in *Young Guns* (1988).
Courtesy of Twentieth Century Fox.

of up-and-coming actors headlined by Brat Pack star Emilio Estevez and his brother, Charlie Sheen, to play the outlaw and his gang. That gang, called the Regulators, included Dermot Mulroney, Casey Siemaszko, Kiefer Sutherland, and Lou Diamond Phillips.

HOW TO GET THERE

Cerrillos is located off New Mexico 14, about thirty minutes south of Santa Fe.

WHERE TO EAT

Black Bird Saloon
28 Main Street
Los Cerrillos, NM 87010
505-438-1821
blackbirdsaloon.com

Young Guns crew members spent three weeks preparing Cerrillos for the film. They added additional buildings and covered the streets with dirt. Some of the paint from the film is still visible. Look for the Wortley Hotel sign while entering town. The real Wortley Hotel is a historic building in Lincoln.

While in Cerrillos, it's worth the short trip to the Cerrillos Hills State Park (37 Main Street, Cerrillos, NM, 87010; 505-474-0196, emnrd.state.nm.us/SPD/cerrilloshillsstatepark.html). The area is littered with the remnants of mines, some of which are hundreds of years old. The park has several miles of hiking trails over mostly gentle slopes. The Cerrillos Turquoise Mining Museum and Casa Grande Trading Post (17 Waldo St, Los Cerrillos, NM, 87010; 505-438-3008, casagrandetradingpost.com) has mining artifacts for sale and on display. There's also a petting zoo.

SELECTED FILMOGRAPHY

Cain, Christopher, dir. *Young Guns*. USA: Twentieth Century Fox, 1988. Film.

Nyby, Christian, dir. *The Magical World of Disney*. Season 5, episode 17, "Elfego Baca, Attorney at Law." Aired February 6, 1959. USA: Walt Disney Productions, 1959. Television episode.

The Mine Shaft Tavern in Madrid. Photo by Amanda Lynn Robinson.

8

MADRID

Once a coal-mining center, Madrid has transformed into New Mexico's most colorful not-quite ghost town. The motorcycle comedy Wild Hogs *built a café façade in the town that has since been converted into a functional gift shop celebrating the film.*

Out of water and out of gasoline, the four middle-aged motorcyclists in *Wild Hogs* crest a hill to find the town of Madrid, an oasis in the desert. As they enter city limits, actor William H. Macy, playing a character named Duncan, instructs his friends on how to properly pronounce the little town's name. Unlike the city in Spain, this name is pronounced *Maaad-rid*. His correction is played for laughs, but it's true.

The four members of the Wild Hogs motorcycle club arrive in the one-road town and quickly gulp up all the water they can find at the local diner. They're temporarily mistaken for a real motorcycle gang, one that will soon lay siege to little Madrid. Macy's character falls in love with the proprietor of the diner, and the four bikers camp out in the little town while they wait for gas. As the Wild Hogs hole up, they indulge in the finest that this fictional version of Madrid has to offer, including carnival games and country dancing at a chile festival.

The actual Madrid is also known for its events. The town hosts several each year, including a Blues Festival, a Gypsy Festival, and concerts at the historic baseball stadium, which has been recently restored. It's a remarkable slate of activities for a town that once all but dried up and disappeared.

The Wild Hogs roll through Madrid (2007). Courtesy of Buena Vista Pictures.

Named after a pioneer family, this funky little enclave was once a successful coal-mining center. From the close of the nineteenth century until the 1950s, Madrid was a model company town and had a store, schools, a hospital, an employee's club, and even a baseball field for a semiprofessional team. The Oscar Huber Memorial Stadium in which the team played was one of the first stadiums in the American West to have lighting for night games.

Madrid's light-filled Christmas celebration was famous throughout the region and is (probably erroneously) credited with inspiring Disney's Parade of Lights. When coal mining stopped there, the town was mostly abandoned until an infusion of artists and counterculture enthusiasts flooded the area beginning in the 1970s. Now, Madrid is a destination for those seeking off-the-grid lifestyles and an artistic vibe.

Madrid and neighboring Cerrillos are highlights of the Turquoise Trail Scenic Byway (turquoisetrail.org). Beginning in Tijeras, just east of Albuquerque, the byway follows New Mexico 14 north to Santa Fe. Complete with great views and fun places to stop, the byway takes about forty-five minutes longer than the more direct I-25 from Albuquerque to Santa Fe. In addition to Cerrillos, Madrid, and the Sandia Mountains (see locations 7, 8, and 27), the route includes the historic town of Golden.

If you follow the byway to Madrid, be sure to stop in at Maggie's Diner (2867 New Mexico State Road 14, Madrid, NM, 87010), whose false store front was built for *Wild Hogs*. It was used for several scenes in a diner run by a character played by Marisa Tomei. After shooting, the production left the false front in place. A steady stream of curious tourists, who didn't quite believe that it wasn't a real restaurant, eventually convinced investors to transform the fake building into a working store that sells film-related paraphernalia.

The climactic fistfight in *Wild Hogs* unravels just feet from this building. The four middle-aged leading men square up against an entire gang of road-tested bikers and get their butts kicked. In a hilarious twist, the Wild Hogs are saved by the last-minute intervention of motorcycling legend Peter Fonda, throwing a wink at the character he played in *Easy Rider*, which shot briefly in Madrid decades before.

If drug culture permeated through *Easy Rider*, it positively burned up the screen in *Greaser's Palace*. This acid western is simultaneously a surreal trip and socially conscientious art piece. Directed by cult filmmaker Robert Downey Sr. and shot around Madrid, the film is a retelling of the Christ story with a Western twist.

For a less abstract high, get drinks at the Mine Shaft Tavern. The rustic, Western-themed bar was built in 1946 on the footprint of a tavern constructed for mine workers a half-century earlier. The tavern often has live music and special events. It's also a useful backdrop for Hollywood productions. It can be seen in episodes of *Longmire*, *Wild Hogs*, and *Paul*. The attached Ghost Town Museum includes artifacts from the town's colorful history and even some displays on films made in the area. There's also live theater and a Mexican restaurant attached to the tavern complex (2846

HOW TO GET THERE

Situated along the Turquoise Trail, Madrid can be reached via New Mexico State Road 14 going north or south.

WHERE TO STAY

See accommodations in Albuquerque or Santa Fe.

WHERE TO EAT

The Hollar
2849 New Mexico State Road 14
Madrid, NM 87010
505-471-4821
thehollar.com

New Mexico State Road 14, Madrid, NM, 87010; 505-473-0743, themineshaft tavern.com).

CREW MEMORY

A colleague and I were surveying a bar, the Mine Shaft Tavern, in Madrid for a miniseries, and halfway through the bartenders informed us that the area in which we were to be filming is notoriously haunted. Apparently, the whole place is a bit spooky, but that corner by the fireplace is particularly known for ghostly activity. They didn't say much more than that, even after we asked for more information. —*Amanda Lynn Robinson, Set Designer*

SELECTED FILMOGRAPHY

Becker, Walt, dir. *Wild Hogs*. USA: Buena Vista Pictures, 2007. Film.

Downey, Robert, Sr., dir. *Greaser's Palace*. USA: Cinema 5 Distributing, 1972. Film.

9

EVANGELO'S COCKTAIL LOUNGE

This vibrant bar, just feet from the Santa Fe Plaza, appeared in the Jeff Bridges film Crazy Heart.

Billing itself as a staple of the Santa Fe nightlife, Evangelo's is a real-life venue for live music. It also happens to appear in film as, not coincidentally, a venue for live music. Most notably, the bar appeared in *Crazy Heart* as a spot where Jeff Bridges's Bad Blake found a little bit of trouble and a big bit of redemption.

Blake, once a renowned country singer, has fallen on hard times. Worst of all, his former protégé, the famous and successful Tommy Sweet (Colin Farrell), won't throw him a bone.

At the start of the film, Blake performs at a run-down bowling alley for pocket cash. He is down to his last few dollars and relies on the kindness of a fan just to get some whiskey. The whiskey, though, is the real problem. Blake is struggling with alcoholism and drinks to such excess that he barely makes it through a single set. Bridges received an Academy Award for his work on the film.

Despite his dangerous benders, Blake is sober enough for several performances at Evangelo's, which stands in for itself as a rocking live-music spot. Prior to the performance, Blake is introduced to an aspiring journalist with whom he develops a relationship. Eventually, Blake's demons spoil the relationship, inspiring the character to write the film's title track, "The Weary Kind," which encapsulates Blake's struggles.

Written by T-Bone Burnett and musician Ryan Bingham, the song was recognized with an Academy Award. Bingham also plays a small role in the film as a band member. Born in New Mexico, Bingham grew up all over the Southwest and competed in rodeos while learning to play the guitar. He broke through with two al-

Jeff Bridges performs in *Crazy Heart* (2009). Courtesy of Fox Searchlight Pictures.

The exterior of Evangelo's as it appears in *Crazy Heart* (2009). Courtesy of Fox Searchlight Pictures.

bums before working with Burnett on the music for *Crazy Heart*. In addition to his cameo in *Crazy Heart*, Bingham reteamed with director Scott Cooper for a scene in *Hostiles* in which he plays a singing soldier.

A few years after filming *Crazy Heart*, Bridges returned to Evangelo's for the firefighter drama *Only the Brave*. Bridges's character is part of a team of elite firefighters having a party at Evangelo's, and Bridges performs onstage again. Almost all of these elite firefighters perish in this dramatization of the real-life events of the 2013 Yarnell Hill Fire in Arizona.

The actual Evangelo's is named after a Greek immigrant who first arrived in Santa Fe in the 1930s. He went on to fight in World War II, perhaps participating in covert operations. After his death, his children investigated this mysterious legacy. Much to their surprise, a photo of their father popped up in a local bookstore. Angelo, it turned out, had been the subject of a famous photograph taken by the celebrated war-chronicler Eugene Smith. The photo now hangs on the outside of the bar. The bar hosts live

HOW TO GET THERE

200 West San Francisco Street
Santa Fe, NM 87501
evangeloscocktaillounge.com

Please note that this bar is cash only.

WHERE TO STAY

Eldorado Hotel & Spa
309 West San Francisco Street
Santa Fe, NM 87501
505-988-4455
eldoradohotel.com

WHERE TO EAT

The Shed
113½ East Palace Avenue
Santa Fe, NM, 87501
505-982-9030
sfshed.com

Few New Mexican joints rival The Shed for reputation or quirkiness.

music several times a week, more often during the busy season. It also has a billiards hall.

SELECTED FILMOGRAPHY

Cooper, Scott, dir. *Crazy Heart*. USA: Fox Searchlight Pictures, 2009. Film.

Kosinski, Joseph, dir. *Only the Brave*. USA: Columbia Pictures, 2017. Film.

10

DIABLO CANYON

The sheer basalt walls in this deep canyon just north of Santa Fe make a dramatic backdrop for period Westerns.

The result of ancient volcanic activity, Diablo Canyon is a narrow channel through walls of basaltic rock. These jet-black cliffs make a dramatic backdrop for hiking, climbing, and filmmaking.

In the 1880s a pioneering lumberjack from Oregon built a bridge across the Rio Grande not far from the canyon. The small town that arose at the site took his name. Buckman soon had a post office and a sawmill, which made it a hub of activity for a while. After the bridge washed away in a storm, though, the town all but went with it. All that remains today are signs for Old Buckman Road—a bumpy, washboard, unpaved affair that winds its way to the canyon from the Santa Fe bedroom community of Las Campanas.

The road, though, is good enough for film crews. Westerns, in particular, enjoy the solitude and stark look of Diablo. In the opening few minutes of the Coen Brothers' *Ballad of Buster Scruggs*, for instance, actor Tim Blake Nelson, playing a singing cowboy, picks and canters his way through Monument Valley and into Diablo Canyon. According to director Ethan Coen, the team "actually saw the canyon—Diablo Canyon—in Santa Fe while scouting another movie and thinking, 'We gotta go back to Diablo Canyon!'"

Hikers who want to get dusty can walk through the canyon for just over four miles on a simple out-and-back. The trail is rocky and exposed, so it's best to bring sturdy shoes and sun attire. Alternatively, the Rio Grande can be reached via several more miles on Old Buckman Road.

Diablo Canyon in *Hostiles* (2017). Courtesy of Waypoint Entertainment.

Diablo Canyon in *The Ballad of Buster Scruggs* (2018). Courtesy of Netflix.

HOW TO GET THERE

Take Camino la Tierra west from New Mexico 599. Continue on Camino la Tierra to Old Buckman Road. Take Old Buckman for about 7.5 miles to the Diablo Canyon parking and camping area.

WHERE TO STAY

Hotel Santa Fe
1501 Paseo de Peralta
Santa Fe, NM 87501
855-825-9876
hotelsantafe.com

Hotel Santa Fe has the unique distinction of Native American ownership. The Pueblo of Picuris is a major investor in the property.

WHERE TO EAT

Arroyo Vino
218 Camino la Tierra
Santa Fe, NM 87506
505-983-2100
arroyovino.com

The real attraction at Diablo Canyon might be the many rock-climbing routes on the cliffs. The canyon is a premier spot for multi-pitch traditional, sport, and top-rope routes. In other words, the rocks offer climbs for almost every skill level. The Santa Fe Climbing Center (3008 Cielo Court, Santa Fe, NM, 87507, 505-986-8944, climbsantafe.com) offers both indoor climbing and guided outdoor trips.

SELECTED FILMOGRAPHY

Coen, Ethan and Joel, dirs. *The Ballad of Buster Scruggs*. USA: Netflix Studios, 2017. Film.

On patrol in *Lone Survivor* (2013). Courtesy of Universal Pictures.

11

SKI SANTA FE

This ski area, just miles from downtown Santa Fe, appeared as Afghanistan in the war drama Lone Survivor.

After World War II, sport savvy Santa Feans moved their local ski area from Hyde Park, only a few miles from town, to a spot higher up the mountain. Their new ski area sat at ten thousand feet above sea level, not far from the summit of Santa Fe Baldy. The new location seemed ideal for more difficult terrain and more consistent snow.

The ski basin employees carved pistes through the steep mountainsides and through multiple glades. Next, they recovered an old mining tram from Silverton, Colorado, to use as a chair lift. The clutch failed spectacularly, but the tram worked well enough. Despite the accidents, the ski area prospered and grew larger. Today, Ski Santa Fe features eighty-three trails over 1,725 vertical feet covering 660 acres.

Thanks to that relatively high altitude and the typically dense snowpack, Ski Santa Fe stays green and lush even after the snowmelt. Coupled with expansive mountain views, the area makes a convenient spot to shoot mountainous scenes. It is also easy to access thanks to a paved road and a wide parking lot just below the slopes.

The military drama *Lone Survivor* used the mountains on the ski basin to sub for the peaks in Afghanistan where real-life Navy SEALs fought for their lives. Peter Berg adapted and directed the film based on the memoir of the same name by Marcus Luttrell. Along with four other SEALS, Luttrell was sent behind enemy lines and was soon surrounded by a much larger Taliban force. Only Luttrell survived.

To prepare the cast, producers hired special forces veterans to direct an intensive bootcamp. Actors underwent several weeks of weapons instructions, physical drills, and lessons in tactical movement. Luttrell himself spent time on set.

With little preamble, the film delves into the harrowing battle scenes, during which the surrounded and outnumbered SEALs find themselves trapped and pinned down. To escape, the SEALs literally jump off one cliff, then tumble from another. The brutal scenes are difficult to watch and were challenging to create.

Ski Santa Fe provided some of the cliffsides for the leaps. Berg said that his cast got a little too into the experience. "Particularly Ben Foster and Taylor Kitsch, I had to keep pulling them off the hill, because they wanted to throw themselves off. A lot of my job was just to tell them, 'You're not going to throw yourself off a twenty-foot cliff.'"

To get the working crew to these remote, alpine locations, the production paid Ski Santa Fe to turn on and run the chair lifts. They also hired some tough locals to act as sherpas and help haul equipment up the mountains on foot. To access other parts of the mountain, the crew used military-grade, six-wheeled transport vehicles that provided a bumpy ride up toward the top of the mountain.

Berg later said about transportation up the ski mountain that "for lunch, Mark Wahlberg would get on a chairlift with everybody else, put an egg salad sandwich in his pocket, and [we'd] give him a piece of equipment, he'd carry it up. It wasn't, 'Okay, we're gonna stop for two hours and have lunch.' There were no chairs up there. There were no vanity squads. One makeup artist would run around and try and keep everybody under control."

Weather allowing, Ski Santa Fe opens every year around Thanksgiving and closes around April. Despite the relatively limited acreage of the basin, the technical quality of the terrain makes the mountain a frequent destination for Santa Feans, many of whom are skilled skiers. The ski area also offers novice runs.

Just a few miles downhill from the ski area parking lot, the Norski Trailhead area is perfect for cross-country skiing. The two-mile trail is marked and easy to follow from the turnoff.

The ski basin is also popular in the summer months, when local trails offer some of the best views of Santa Fe and Northern New Mexico. The Winsor Trail, just below the Ski Santa Fe parking lot, is one of the better-known and most popular paths in the Sangre de Cristos Mountains. It provides access to several secluded lakes.

A few miles down-mountain from the ski area is the extremely popular Aspen Vista Trail (off Hyde Park Rd, Santa Fe, NM, 87506). During fall, the trail fills up with Santa Fe locals who come to see the aspen tree leaves change from green to brilliant yellow. The easy-to-follow path eventually works its way into the ski basin.

Both hikers and skiers should be prepared for thin air and the rapidly changing conditions, common on mountains that reach ten thousand feet in elevation. Hikers typically start their day early so that they can be off the mountain by the time afternoon thunderstorms roll through.

CREW MEMORY

We were doing a night shoot at the Santa Fe Ski basin in late September, and an hour or two into our day—around 9:00 p.m.—a lightning storm rolled in. We waited out our first lightning delay and went back to set only to have another lightning delay called. It seemed like it went on like that all night—every thirty minutes or so, just as we were back in, there would be another lightning strike and another delay. Eventually a few cast and crew piled into one of the cast SUVs to wait out the storm. It was sometime around 1:00 a.m., probably. The song "November Rain" came on the radio, and our actress told us to turn it up. Someone—not telling who—broke out a bottle of chocolate-flavored whisky, and we passed it around. We read each other's tarot cards. Another lightning delay was called. I think we finally got something on film just an hour or two before dawn. —Anonymous

SELECTED FILMOGRAPHY

Berg, Peter, dir. *Lone Survivor*. USA: Universal Pictures, 2013. Film.

HOW TO GET THERE

New Mexico State Road 475
Santa Fe, NM 87501
505-982-4429
skisantafe.com

WHERE TO STAY

Ten Thousand Waves
21 Ten Thousand Waves Way
Santa Fe, NM 87501
505-982-9304
tenthousandwaves.com

Only a few miles up Artist Road from downtown Santa Fe, Ten Thousand Waves is a Japanese-style bathhouse and one of the premiere spa and massage destinations in New Mexico. It's where film-crew members go to relax after long shoots. The spa has individual pools, community bathing, and massages.

WHERE TO EAT

Izanami
21 Ten Thousand Waves Way
Santa Fe, NM 87501
505-428-6409
tenthousandwaves.com

This Japanese-inspired restaurant attached to Ten Thousand Waves has an excellent selection of sake.

12

TESUQUE VILLAGE AND PUEBLO

The Jemez Mountains provide the backdrop for the historic pueblo and the nearby Santa Fe Opera.

Just north of Santa Fe are two communities called Tesuque. One is a Native American Pueblo and the other a more recent suburb of Santa Fe. Tesuque Pueblo is roughly eight hundred years old. Tesuque Village is much younger, established around 1732.

The people of Tesuque moved into their current location sometime around 1300 CE. Later, residents played a pivotal role in the Pueblo Revolt of 1680. Not only were they responsible for delivering the knotted cords used as a sort of calendar to announce the revolt, Tesuque warriors also delivered some of the first blows in the rebellion.

Following the Pueblo Revolt, the population of Tesuque dwindled. Tesuque was resettled during the 1690s and took some of its present shape with its central plaza built around a mission. Originally built in 1745, the mission had all but crumbled to the ground when the people of Tesuque reconstructed it in the 1880s for religious use. The new mission had a simple adobe facade with a Territorial-style window. Standing over the plaza at the center of Tesuque, the mission makes for a picturesque backdrop for film and photos.

The plaza and the mission are clearly visible in *The Man from Laramie* as Jimmy Stewart makes a foray into town. The plaza also pops up in *The Texas Rangers*, a 1936 film directed by King Vidor and based on the book by Western author and historian Walter Prescott Webb.

The Camel Rock (285 Frontage Road, Santa Fe, NM, 87506), a weathered stone formation right off US Route 84/285, made a

Jimmy Stewart, John War Eagle, and Alex Nicol at Tesuque in *The Man from Laramie*,
© 1955 (renewed 1983) by Columbia Pictures Industries, Inc. All Rights Reserved.
Courtesy of Columbia Pictures and the Paul Andrew Hutton Collection.

Fred MacMurray at Tesuque Pueblo in *The Texas Rangers* (1936).
Courtesy of the Paul Andrew Hutton Collection and Paramount Pictures.

star turn in *Greaser's Palace*. It looks exactly like a Middle Eastern dromedary and is hard to miss from the road. A small parking area provides a good spot for photos. Across the street, the former site of the Camel Rock Casino is now a mixed-use film warehouse and studio. It's not open to the public.

The Santa Fe Opera, also visible from the highway, is a nationally renowned venue for live performances. The opera held its first rendition of Puccini's *Madame Butterfly* in 1957 and has hosted acclaimed talent from all over the world almost every summer since. Prior to performances, operagoers hold extravagant tailgates that put their football watching counterparts to shame. Tickets often sell quickly, so it's best to plan ahead for shows of interest.

In the climatic moments of *Crazy Heart*, the opera house is the backdrop for Bad Blake's triumphant return. Sober and clean-cut, Blake has accepted his role as a songwriter for Tommy Sweet and profited from the work. He meets up with his old flame and hands her a check that atones for some of his sins.

It takes only a few minutes to reach the opera via the highway, but the drive through nearby Tesuque Village is worth the extra time. This wooded, green valley is home to a handful of art galleries and some fun local markets filled with great food and kitsch for tourists

HOW TO GET THERE

To reach the Pueblo, take US Route 84/285 North and take the exit for County Road, then take the Frontage Road north to NP 806 and take a left. NP 806 goes directly into the Pueblo and makes a loop around the plaza.

To reach the Village, take Bishop's Lodge Road out of central Santa Fe.

The opera is accessible via US Route 84/285. Proceed to the Opera Drive exit and take a left.

WHERE TO STAY

Four Seasons Resort Rancho Encantado Santa Fe
198 State Road 592
Santa Fe, NM 87506
505-946-5700
fourseasons.com/santafe

WHERE TO EAT

Tesuque Village Market (TVM)
138 Tesuque Village Road
Santa Fe, NM 87506
505-988-8848
tesuquevillagemarket.com

A true country market, TVM sells basic groceries and baked goods. The restaurant has a wood-fired oven and specializes in pizzas and New Mexican fare.

PART III

NORTHERN NEW MEXICO

Bandelier National Monument. Photo by Gerd Eichmann, © CC by SA 4.0 via Wikimedia Commons.

13

BANDELIER NATIONAL MONUMENT

These historic homes carved into soft volcanic cliffs appeared in the underground hit Billy Jack.

First inhabited around 1150 CE, the Ancestral Puebloans who lived at Bandelier took advantage of the natural landscape when they carved their homes into the soft, volcanic rock of Frijoles Canyon. In addition to their remarkable cliff dwellings, they also built multistoried villages in the center of the canyons and atop the mesas. The Ancestral Pueblo peoples left the massive structures at Bandelier around 1550 CE, likely due to resource scarcity, and moved closer to the fertile Rio Grande, but the structures remain.

A European archaeologist named Adolph Bandelier first visited the Frijoles Canyon in 1880. What he saw there captured his imagination. Bandelier studied the area extensively and published his findings. He helped popularize Native American architecture in the Southwest and boosted international interest in the region's history. The national monument was eventually named in his honor.

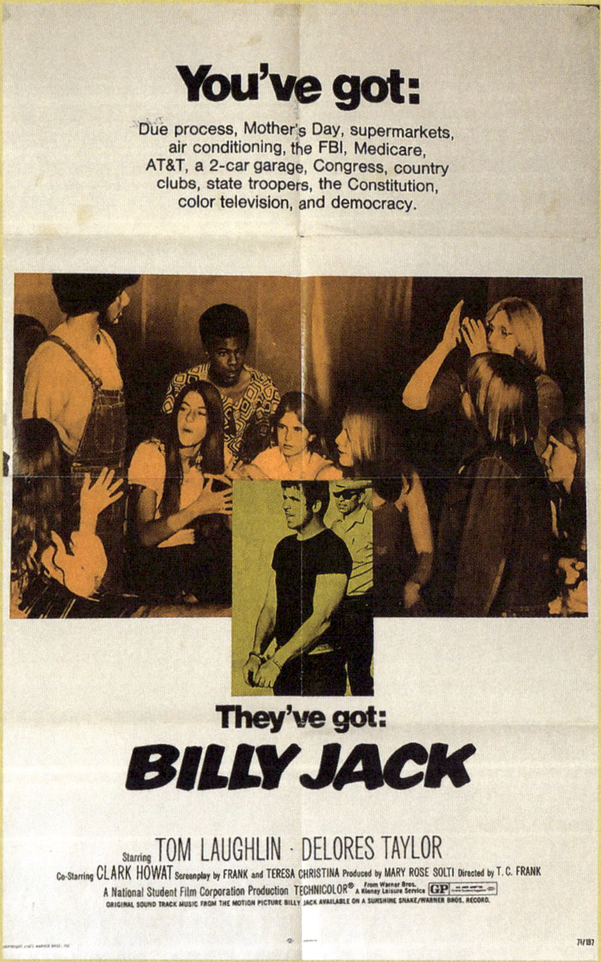

Poster for *Billy Jack* (1971) promoting the film's social-justice sensibility. Courtesy of the Paul Andrew Hutton Collection.

Because the national monument is Federally protected, it's relatively rare to see it used on film. Somehow, the producers of the underground hit *Billy Jack* gained access and shot an integral, surreal sequence in the heart of the national monument among the ruins of a massive pueblo.

A sequel to the motorcycle-gang flick *The Born Losers*, *Billy Jack* is a pulpy, punchy action film with heavy cultural overtones. The title character, played by the film's director, Tom Laughlin, is a Native American hapkido (a Korean martial art) expert who served in the Green Berets and then returned home. Jack patrols the reservation enforcing a kind of vigilante justice and combating racism.

On one such patrol he comes across a pregnant teenage girl who has been beaten and thrown to the side of the road. Jack takes her to a local hospital only to discover that the girl's father is a local sheriff and is responsible for her beating. Jack hides the girl at a local alternative school. Soon, her father causes mayhem searching for her, and Billy Jack is swept up in the chaos.

In an effort to refocus his purpose and mission, Jack holds a snakebite ceremony. Supposedly, the snake's venom will help Jack have a vision and then understand what to do next. The scene was shot at the remains of Tyuonyi Pueblo in Frijoles Canyon, just feet from the Bandelier National Monument Visitor's Center. An expert on the ceremony was hired to advise the producers, and dancers were brought in from Taos Pueblo.

The original release of *Billy Jack* failed to turn heads at the box office, but Laughlin wanted to test another approach. He sued Warner Bros. for the right to rerelease the film his way. In 1971 he ordered 1,200 prints of the film and had them sent to a corresponding number of screens in theaters he booked. Typically, prints cycled through multiple theaters, making the release process more deep than wide. Laughlin's wide release of *Billy Jack* pushed word of mouth on the film and prompted the movie to make a massive box-office splash. The sequel to *Billy Jack* also

HOW TO GET THERE

15 Entrance Road
Los Alamos, NM 87544
505-672-3861 x0
nps.gov/band

WHERE TO STAY

The Juniper Family Campground is a developed site with running water, toilets, and picnic tables.

15 Entrance Road
Los Alamos, NM 87544
877-444-6777
www.nps.gov/band/planyourvisit/juniper-family-campground.htm

If campgrounds aren't for you, nearby Los Alamos has several chain motels and hotels.

WHERE TO EAT

Sirphey at Bandelier
1793 Deacon Street
Los Alamos, NM 87544
505-661-4003
sirphey.com

The restaurant serves classic New Mexican dishes adjacent to the Visitor's Center.

went boffo at the box office. Unbelievably, it bested Francis Ford Coppola's *Godfather Part II* in receipts that year.

Laughlin's strange career included yet one more *Billy Jack* film and a few unsuccessful runs for president of the United States. He and his wife, Delores Taylor, at one point managed their own Montessori school in Los Angeles. The school ultimately went bankrupt, but their collective belief in alternative teaching methods and the importance of education is on display in *Billy Jack*.

Bandelier is home to a museum and several hiking trails all readily accessible from the Visitor's Center. A short trail behind the center winds through Tyuonyi Pueblo and into the cliff dwellings. A longer, relatively flat trail leads to the Alcove House farther down the canyon. Deeper still into the backcountry is Yapashi Pueblo. The fourteen-mile hike to this large complex yields impressive views of several canyons and is an expert-level trek.

A satellite section of the monument called Tsankawi is an oft-missed gem. Not contiguous to the other thirty-three thousand square acres of Bandelier, Tsankawi can be reached on the road to the town of White Rock (New Mexico State Road 4, just past the junction for New Mexico State Road 502). A short hike along an ancient trail encompasses a small mesa and yields sweeping views. Tsankawi Pueblo sits atop the mesa and is strewn with pottery sherds and other remnants of Pueblo life. (All of these artifacts are protected by Federal law. It is illegal to take souvenirs from the landscape.)

SELECTED FILMOGRAPHY

Laughlin, Tom, dir. *Billy Jack*. USA: Warner Bros., 1971. Film.

Lobby card from *The Atomic City* (1952). Courtesy of the Paul Andrew Hutton Collection and Paramount Pictures.

14

LOS ALAMOS AND ENVIRONS

The abduction thriller The Atomic City *was shot in the real home of the atomic bomb.*

Before World War II, Los Alamos was a sleepy ranch town best known as the home of a summer boys' camp. Physicist Robert Oppenheimer changed that when he selected the isolated hamlet as the top-secret location for Project Y, later known as the Manhattan Project. Almost immediately, Los Alamos transformed into the covert, but buzzing, center of American atomic science.

Rather famously, Los Alamos was so secretive that to reach it visitors had to start at a nondescript location in downtown Santa Fe known simply as 109 East Palace Avenue. From there, visitors were shuttled over the Rio Grande and up to the "Hill." Only after the War, and the successful detonation of the atomic bomb in Hiroshima and Nagasaki, did the work at Los Alamos become public knowledge.

It didn't take long for Hollywood to come knocking. In 1952 *The Atomic City* used Los Alamos as a fictional and actual backdrop for a kidnapping and detective yarn. The film begins with an explanation of work done at Los Alamos and accompanying footage of scientific laboratories that set the stage for a mysterious drama. The child of a nuclear physicist working at the lab is abducted, and the physicist is soon swallowed up in intrigue. It's cloak and dagger all the way, with the fate of national security on the line.

Bits of stock footage appear to be the only segments actually made in Los Alamos. Most of the film was shot on stages in Los Angeles. Regardless, the footage and the film itself are both early interpretations of Los Alamos life.

In the 1980s, director Mike Nichols filmed the Academy Award–

nominated drama *Silkwood* partially in Los Alamos along with locations elsewhere in New Mexico and Texas. The film is about a real-life, contaminated plutonium plant worker and stars Meryl Streep, Cher, and Kurt Russell.

Decades later, the television show *Manhattan* focused on the intrigue in the lives of fictionalized versions of several key Project Y scientists. The series used an old World War II barracks in central Santa Fe to recreate the campus at Los Alamos as it would have appeared at that time. (These historic buildings later burned in a fire. The nearby Greer Garson Stages are still in use as of press time.) Other segments of *Manhattan* shot at Bonanza Creek Ranch, including a recreation of the Trinity Test Site that featured an accurate reconstruction of the "gadget" itself. Despite the fact that the production shot in the same state as the site of the actual test and the actual labs, filming always requires permits and access, making some locations all but impossible. Los Alamos National Laboratory, as it is still an operating DOD and DOE facility, is not amenable to Hollywood productions.

While Los Alamos is best known for the Lab, it has a lot more to offer. For instance, campers at the pre–World War II Los Alamos Ranch School developed a skiing spot close to town. GIs and scientists contributed to the skiing fervor during the days of the Manhattan Project. In 1957, ski enthusiasts moved their community lifts and operation to Pajarito Mountain. The mountain is now owned by a local conglomeration of ski resorts.

Like Ski Santa Fe, Pajarito makes a conveniently accessible mountain for filming. The mountain is also a little more flexible in allowing high-impact shooting activities. For the firefighting drama *Only the Brave*, special-effects technicians rigged and staged forest fires along some of the access roads up the mountain. And Westerns like *The Lone Ranger* have used Pajarito for its dramatic and unspoiled views.

Los Alamos is still an active research facility and is kept under tight security. Visitors should be prepared to speak with guards at a checkpoint going into town. But don't be dissuaded—the Atomic

City has a lot to do.

The Bradbury Science Museum (1350 Central Avenue, Los Alamos, NM, 87544; 505-667-4444, lanl.gov/museum/) gives an excellent overview of the development and consequences of the bomb. The Los Alamos History Museum (1050 Bathtub Row, Los Alamos, NM, 87544; 505-662-4493, losalamoshistory.org) packs in information about several eras of the local past including the pioneer era, the Ranch School years, the Ancestral Pueblo period, and the time of the Manhattan Project.

The National Park Service integrated three properties that were once part of the Manhattan Project sites into a single historical park. The Park Service administers property at Oak Ridge, Tennessee; Hanford, Washington; and Los Alamos. The Visitors Center (475 20th Street, Los Alamos, NM, 87544; 505-661-6277, nps.gov/mapr/) in Los Alamos includes an introductory video and directions for a walking tour of the city.

WHERE TO STAY

Los Alamos has several chain motels and hotels.

WHERE TO EAT

Blue Window Bistro
1789 Central Avenue
Los Alamos, NM 87544
505-662-6305
labluewindowbistro.com

CREW MEMORY

Scout work for the Angelina Jolie film *Those Who Wish Me Dead* (written and directed by Taylor Sheridan) began in a very heavy snowfall the January before the show was set to begin filming that spring. Mountaintops needed for scenes in this neo-Western thriller were waist deep in snow. Producers and designers had to use their imagination to picture what nearby mountain meadows would look like come spring. The always accommodating Pajarito Ski Area manager Tommy Long (and his well-known, cigar-chomping dad, Tom Long) offered to haul our entire scout team up to the top of the mountain in their snow cat. With snowshoes and poles, ten members of the team piled into the rear cage of the cat while I rode shotgun with Tommy. I'm not saying I enjoyed it, but (!) riding up front while all the above-the-liners were locked up out back brought me a nice grin. "Should I take the long way around or freak them out by going straight up?" Tommy asked.

"Straight up!" was my reply! —*Cyndy McCrossen, Location Scout*

SELECTED FILMOGRAPHY

Hopper, Jerry, dir. *The Atomic City*. USA: Paramount Pictures, 1952. Film.

Kosinski, Joseph, dir. *Only the Brave*. USA: Columbia Pictures, 2017. Film.

15

VALLES CALDERA NATIONAL PRESERVE

Walt Longmire's cabin is nestled in this green, sprawling valley, deep in an old volcano, for the A+E Network television show Longmire.

Just over a million years ago, a large volcano in the Jemez Mountains erupted. The mountain spread ash and lava flow all over the immediate area, creating the soft, swiss-cheesy topsoil that is so prevalent in the region. The eruption also caused the roof of the volcano to collapse, resulting in one of the largest volcanic craters in the world, now called Valles Caldera, which sits along the volcanic arcs of the Jemez Lineament and the Rio Grande Rift.

Over time, the interior of the crater eroded and settled into a series of contiguous grassland valleys. This lush basin is still filled with elk, bear, and deer. The Pueblo people used the area as a hunting ground and to gather obsidian left by the volcano, which they used for projectile points and tools. More recently, ranchers and loggers tried to take advantage of the Caldera's natural assets before the National Park Service stepped in to take control. The Park Service has taken strict measures to protect the fragile ecosystem in what is now the Valles Caldera National Preserve.

That same ecosystem is also valuable to filmmakers. While much of New Mexico is parched high desert, the Valles Caldera is reliably green and filled with foliage. Coupled with the mountain views, the area is an obvious attraction for filmmakers.

In search of a hit, actor Gregory Peck connected with part of the creative team from *True Grit* (1969) to film in Valles Caldera.

Walt Longmire's cabin in the Valles Caldera in *Longmire* (2012–2017). Courtesy of Netflix.

(The John Wayne adaptation of the Charles Portis novel shot in Ridgway, Colorado, but the Coen Brothers adaptation shot partially in New Mexico.) The result was a revenge thriller called *Shoot Out* for which the crew built a small Western town in the valley.

Several other projects made additions to the caldera. For the television series *Buffalo Girls* starring Anjelica Huston and Melanie Griffith, the crew built a faux Western town, part of which is still standing. A decade later, a pioneer's cabin and barn were built close to the entrance of the preserve for the motion picture *The Missing*. The Ron Howard–directed frontier thriller starred Cate Blanchett and Tommy Lee Jones.

A little deeper into the caldera, fans of the television drama *Longmire* will recognize Walt Longmire's cabin among a cluster of historic buildings. Based on a series of novels by Craig Johnson, the show follows the sheriff of a fictional county in Wyoming. An homage to classic Western lawmen, Longmire enforces justice with a relentless moral code.

The show commanded good ratings, but A+E Network decided to cancel it because the viewership skewed toward older fans who are not prized by advertisers. Almost immediately after the bad news broke, the studio behind the show began shopping it to new networks and platforms. Passionate fans helped by forming an online "Longmire Posse" to demonstrate their loyalty. It also helped that about 6 million people had regularly tuned into the show. Netflix purchased the show and brought it back for two more seasons. The show had offices in Santa Fe for its five seasons and filmed all over Northern New Mexico, particularly in Los Alamos and Las Vegas, but the vista shots billed as Wyoming are mainly the green spaces of the Valles Caldera.

Long considered a pre-

HOW TO GET THERE

Take New Mexico State Road 4 to mile marker 39.

WHERE TO STAY AND EAT

Nearest services are in Los Alamos.

mier destination for elk hunting, the preserve allows permits for the sport. About three thousand elk regularly inhabit the preserve and are often visible on the road to the Visitor's Center. Turkey hunting and trout fishing are allowed as well. Fishing for trout is a year-round activity on the multiple rivers and creeks that crisscross the caldera.

The caldera also has a series of hiking trails that checker the big valley. During the winter, snowshoeing and cross-country skiing are available when the snow accumulates. The Visitor's Center offers multiple guided tours, including one that details the history of filming in the area.

SELECTED FILMOGRAPHY

Baldwin, Hunt, and John Coveny, creators. *Longmire*. USA: A+E Network / Netflix, 2012–2017. Television series.

Hathaway, Henry, dir. *Shoot Out*. USA: Universal Pictures, 1971. Film.

Howard, Ron, dir. *The Missing*. USA: Columbia Pictures, 2003. Film.

16

GILMAN TUNNELS AND FENTON LAKE

These rough rock openings, high up in a steep canyon, appeared in 3:10 to Yuma.

The Gilman Tunnels are a short set of openings carved into the rock of a box canyon high up in the Jemez Mountains. Railroaders blasted the tunnels open in 1923 to give trains a delivery route for lumber from the forests to a sawmill in Bernalillo. At first, the tunnel could only accommodate trains, but a flood washed out part of the track farther south, and it could no longer support the railway. The tunnels were widened to allow trucks to pass through when that method of transportation came into vogue.

The rough-hewn rock walls of the tunnels have something of an aged quality, making them perfect for Westerns. The remake of *3:10 to Yuma* (the original film was released in 1957, and the remake in 2007) used the tunnels for a shoot-'em-up chase scene. To make the openings look more period appropriate, the crew covered the now-paved road with dirt. The film is an adaptation of the Elmore Leonard short story of the same name.

Nearby Jemez Historic Site (18160 New Mexico 4, Jemez Springs, NM, 87025; 575-829-3530; nmhistoricsites.org/jemez) is an impressive and sprawling remnant of the Spanish Colonial era. Built around 1621, much of the cathedral and attendant housing is still standing. After the Spanish left in 1640, most of the Pueblo people moved down to the site of their current home, the Pueblo of Jemez. The main village is called Walatowa. The Pueblo has a welcome center and museum that opens to tourists most of the year (7413 New Mexico 4, Jemez Pueblo, NM, 87024; 575-834-7359, jemezpueblo.org).

The town of Jemez Springs is not named idly and has a few natural hot springs. Some are accessible via short hikes while others

The Gilman Tunnels in *3:10 to Yuma* (2007). Courtesy of Lionsgate.

are in commercial venues. The Jemez Springs Bath House (62 Jemez Springs Plaza, Jemez Springs, NM, 87025; 575-829-3303, jemezsprings bathhouse.com) is over a century old and is a registered state historic site. It features mineral baths and massages. For the less-commercial feel, Spence Hot Springs and San Antonio Hot Springs are both reachable by short hikes. These primitive hot springs are quite popular. They are best reached in the summer and fall and are clothing optional.

Not far from the Gilman Tunnels, Fenton Lake State Park contains an alpine body of water complete with stocked trout fishing and camping. David Bowie's character in *The Man Who Fell to Earth* crash lands in the lake and then goes back after he has amassed his fortune. The lake becomes his mountain hideaway and the place he goes to reveal his true self to his lover.

HOW TO GET THERE

Gilman Tunnels
Forest Service Road 376
Jemez Pueblo, NM 87024

Fenton Lake State Park
455 Fenton Lake Road
Jemez Springs, NM 87025
575-829-3630
emnrd.state.nm.us/SPD/fenton lakestatepark.html

WHERE TO STAY

Jemez Hot Springs
040 Abousleman Loop
Jemez Springs, NM 87025
575-829-9175
jemezhotsprings.com

WHERE TO EAT

Los Ojos Restaurant & Saloon
17596 NM-4, Jemez Springs, NM 87025
575-829-3547
losojossaloon.com

SELECTED FILMOGRAPHY

Mangold, James, dir. *3:10 to Yuma*. USA: Lionsgate, 2007. Film.

Roeg, Nicolas, dir. *The Man Who Fell to Earth*. UK: British Lion Film Corporation, 1976. Film.

Plaza Blanca in *Logan* (2017). Courtesy of Twentieth Century Fox.

17

PLAZA BLANCA AND ABIQUIÚ

The ghostly, white sandstone spires of Plaza Blanca made an otherworldly backdrop for the comic-book film Logan.

Spanish settlers built a community atop the ruins of an Ancestral Pueblo village in the early eighteenth century. It came to be known as Abiquiú, a Spanish bastardization of the Native Tewa name for the chokecherry trees that grew abundantly there. Many of the settlers were *Genízaros*, or soldiers of varying ethnic backgrounds, often including detribalized Native Americans. The small town distinguished itself through conflict with neighboring Plains Indians and by holding what were arguably the last major witchcraft trials in North America (1756–1766).

The Saint Thomas the Apostle Catholic Parish church in Abiquiú, designed by John Gaw Meem, made an appearance in the adaptation of the classic novel *Bless Me, Ultima*. Written by educator and native New Mexican Rudolfo Anaya, the novel brought Chicano literature to the mainstream. A coming of age tale about a young boy who seeks the wisdom of a local curandera, the book explored Chicano faith and community. It took decades to adapt, but a film finally got underway in 2010 and used locations all over the state.

A naturalized New Mexican, Georgia O'Keeffe bought her home in Abiquiú in 1945, after years of visiting the area. It was in poor shape and she set about restoring it. Within a few years she made it her primary residence. O'Keeffe lived in Abiquiú until a few years before her death. She turned the place into a lively artists' community, regularly inviting guests from all of the world to stay in New Mexico and create with her for weeks or months at a time.

The biopic *Georgia O'Keeffe*, based on O'Keeffe's life, received

HOW TO GET THERE

Abiquiú and Plaza Blanca are both reachable via US Route 84/285.

Tours of the O'Keeffe Home are available through the O'Keeffe Welcome Center, part of the Georgia O'Keeffe Museum (21120 US Route 84, Abiquiú, NM, 87510; 505-946-1000, okeeffemuseum.org) based in Santa Fe. Check ahead for availably and times.

To reach Plaza Blanca from Abiquiú, go north on US Route 84/285. Turn right on New Mexico State Road 554 and follow it for just over three miles. Drive past the gate for Dar al Islam Mosque and Education Center. Go another half mile to signs for Dar al Islam, then hang a right to a small parking clearing. Dar al Islam owns the neighboring land, including Plaza Blanca, but welcomes visitors. The hike into the plaza is only about a quarter of a mile.

WHERE TO STAY

Abiquiu Inn
21120 U.S. Route 84
Abiquiú, NM 87510
505-685-4378
abiquiuinn.com

Plaza Blanca and the nearby Rio Chama are frequently used by filmmakers, and the Abiquiu Inn is almost always the hotel used by the crew.

WHERE TO EAT

Bode's
21196 US Route 84
Abiquiú, NM 87510
505-685-4422
bodes.com

At first glance, Bode's appears to be a simple gas station. Inside it is a full general store with a wealth of merchandise and a short-order eatery.

permission to shoot in the historic building. At the time, it was the only film ever to do so. Directed by character actor Bob Balaban, the film follows O'Keeffe's ascension to artistic fame and focuses on her turbulent relationship with photographer Alfred Stieglitz.

As a painter, O'Keefe had a fondness for the "white place," a series of canyons known to others as Plaza Blanca. The subject appears often in her work. Part of the Abiquiú rock formation, the cliffs of Plaza Blanca are made of ancient sediments and eroded volcanic ash. The stark look of the area attracts scores of Westerns wanting to take advantage of the unique landscape. *Comanche Moon*, *The Lone Ranger*, and *3:10 to Yuma* are just a few of the films that feature the ghostly formations.

In the genre mashup *Cowboys & Aliens*, for example, the titular aliens park their spacecraft among the spires of Plaza Blanca. The film is director Jon Favreau's attempt at a classic Western—just with aliens. Unfortunately for the filmmakers, the audience had the first impression that the film was a comedy. Favreau spent a lot of time attempting to convince filmgoers that the movie was actually an action adventure. But despite major star power and a crack producing team, the film underperformed at the box office.

The more successful film *Logan* also shot at Plaza Blanca. The white cliffs are the starting point for a frantic escape in this Marvel comic book adaptation. Filmmakers shot the plaza and then digitally added a range of mountains to make it appear as if the plaza is just miles from the Canadian border; just another instance of the diverse New Mexican landscape standing in for parts elsewhere.

SELECTED FILMOGRAPHY

Balaban, Bob, dir. *Georgia O'Keeffe*. USA: Sony Pictures Television, 2009. TV movie.

Favreau, Jon, dir. *Cowboys & Aliens*. USA: Universal Studios, 2011. Film.

Franklin, Carl, dir. *Bless Me, Ultima*. USA: Arenas Entertainment, 2012. Film.

Mangold, James, dir. *Logan*. USA: Twentieth Century Fox, 2017. Film.

The British Army with Santa Clara Pueblo's Black Mesa in the distance in *The Light That Failed* (1939). Courtesy of the Paul Andrew Hutton Collection and Paramount Pictures.

18

PUYE CLIFFS AND SANTA CLARA PUEBLO

These ancient cliff dwellings appeared in a controversial film about Native Americans.

Similar to Bandelier National Monument, Puye Cliffs is a collection of cave dwellings carved into a mesa made of volcanic ash. The structures were inhabited from around 1000 CE to around 1600 CE, virtually the same time period as those at Bandelier. And just like at Bandelier, the Ancestral Pueblo peoples abandoned their cliff dwellings and moved down the valley to be closer to the Rio Grande. The residents of modern-day Santa Clara are closely related to the people who lived at Puye Cliffs.

Privately owned by the Santa Clara Pueblo, Puye Cliffs and much of the surrounding land has proved film friendly for almost a century.

Both Lucille Ball and her daughter shot romantic comedies at Santa Clara Pueblo. In *Valley of the Sun*, Ball plays the betrothed of a crooked Indian Agent. She falls for a morally driven soldier, and hijinks ensue. In *Second Thoughts*,

Lucie Arnaz plays a woman who changes her mind about potential suitors after she becomes pregnant.

Sequences of a film called *Flap* shot at Santa Clara Pueblo and Puye some years later. An adaptation of the novel *Nobody Loves a Drunken Indian*, the film follows a Native American who wants to better conditions for his people but struggles with drinking. He launches several harebrained schemes to take back Native land, which all fail miserably. Ostensibly a comedy of errors, the film skewers the American Indian Movement, which aimed to address issues of systemic poverty and police brutality against people of Native American descent. The movement ultimately reached its public zenith when members captured and occupied Alcatraz Island near San Francisco in 1969. For punchlines, *Flap* descends into potentially racist tropes.

For *Hostiles*, the production used land owned by Santa Clara, just past the cliff dwellings, for several sequences. The shooting site alternately became a hunter's camp, a river crossing, a traveling camp, and a killing site. To stage a climactic scene at one of the camps, the production set up artificial rain makers that sprinkled water into one of the canyons all night.

Puye Cliffs can only be viewed as part of a tour experience, several of which are available. Local guides can take guests to the lower-lying dwellings or to the Pueblo atop the mesa. Guests can also opt to view both as part of an extended tour.

Tickets can be purchased at the Harvey House Exhibit Hall at the bottom of the mesa. Built by the Fred Harvey Company and used for the Indian Detours program, the restored building has exhibits on the history and culture of Puye and Santa Clara Pueblo.

The Puye Cliffs Harvey House is one of more than a dozen such buildings in New Mexico constructed by the Fred Harvey Company for travelers and tourist on the Atchison, Topeka and Santa Fe Railroad. The architecture of these buildings drew on the heritage of the Southwest, embracing Spanish, Mexican, and Native American design. The Harvey Company itself was famous for their service and fresh food, which they brought in constantly on the rail. The women who worked at these railways stops were immortalized in the Judy Garland film *The Harvey Girls*, which wasn't shot in New Mexico.

Nearby Black Mesa is a prominent landmark in the lowlands of Santa Clara Pueblo. Once part of an ancient volcano, the solitary monolith is now a sacred site for the people of Santa Clara. It appeared in the film *Sudan*, in which New Mexico subbed in for Africa.

The Black Mesa Golf Course (15 State Road 399, La Mesilla, NM, 87532; 505-367-4700, golfblackmesa.com), on the edge of Santa Clara Pueblo, sports greens and fairways nestled into steep bluffs and mesas.

HOW TO GET THERE

From Española, take New Mexico State Road 30 to New Mexico State Road 5 to Santa Clara Canyon Road.

Puye Cliffs Welcome Center
300 New Mexico State Road 30
Los Alamos, NM 87532
505-917-6650
puyecliffdwellings.com

WHERE TO STAY

Santa Claran Hotel and Casino
460 North Riverside Drive
Española, NM 87532
877-505-4949
santaclaran.com

Owned by the Pueblo but located in neighboring Española, this hotel is frequently used by production shooting in Northern New Mexico. The casino also appeared in several episodes of *Longmire*.

WHERE TO EAT

El Parasol
603 Santa Cruz Road
Española, NM 87532
505-753-8852
elparasol.com

CREW MEMORY

For the first season of *Cosmos* we recreated village life at Puye and had hundreds of people dressed in traditional clothes. It was crazy. —*Ashley Watson, Producer*

SELECTED FILMOGRAPHY

Reed, Carol, dir. *Flap*. USA: Warner Bros., 1970. Film.
Turman, Lawrence, dir. *Second Thoughts*. USA: Universal Pictures, Associated Film Distribution, 1983. Film.

19

CUMBRES & TOLTEC SCENIC RAILROAD (C&TSRR)

This historic train is one of the biggest stars of New Mexico filmmaking.

General William Jackson Palmer received the Medal of Honor for his efforts during a Civil War battle in Red Hill, Alabama. After the war, he went west in search of opportunity and helped bring the Kansas-Pacific Railroad to Denver. After spending a little time in the mountains, Palmer came to realize that there was great potential in narrow-gauge railroads that could more easily work their way through the high country.

Palmer, along with a partner, founded the Denver & Rio Grande Railroad. Part of the rail spanned from Antonito, Colorado, into the San Juan Mountains to serve the booming mines at Silverton, Colorado. They had hopes of driving a line to El Paso and into Mexico and wanted to construct six branches along the main railway, but they encountered difficulties in expanding through the territory.

To reach Chama, New Mexico, the rail line would have to travel over mountainous terrain at high elevation. Thanks to the grueling nature of the work and the isolated route, labor was difficult to procure. Even so, workers drove the narrow-gauge over a summit at ten thousand feet and completed that stretch in 1880.

Economic recessions, the competition of the Atchison, Topeka & Santa Fe Railroad, and the plummeting cost of silver all combined to doom the Denver & Rio Grande project. Save for the occasional boom, the rail limped into the twentieth century just barely doing business. Palmer's grandiose plans were never completed,

The Cumbres & Toltec Scenic Railroad in *Indiana Jones and The Last Crusade* (1989). Courtesy of Paramount Pictures.

Historic locomotive and 1880 vintage passenger cars on the Cumbres & Toltec Scenic Railroad. Courtesy of the Cumbres & Toltec Scenic Railroad.

and in 1969 the then-owners of the Denver & Rio Grande Railroad sought to abandon the business altogether. Much of the railway was torn up almost immediately.

Concerned citizens, rail fans, and the states of Colorado and New Mexico pitched in to save the most scenic stretch of the railroad. They purchased the track and affiliated structures for half a million dollars and began to restore it as a scenic route. The result of their work is a sixty-four-mile stretch of rail that begins at Chama and ends at Antonito. They renamed it the Cumbres & Toltec Scenic Railroad.

Almost immediately, productions sought out the C&TSRR for its period look and functional nineteenth-century steam engine. Some twenty-seven different productions over the years have made use of the railroad. The antique mechanisms and the mountainous views are ideal for period films. "You will see the world the way it looked 140 years ago," said president of the C&TSRR John Bush. "It's an amazing time capsule," as most of the trains and equipment were built before 1920.

The newest acquisition by the C&TSRR—added to the fleet in 2018–2019—is actually the enterprise's first film star. Engine #168 was built in 1863 and appeared in the film *The Texas Rangers* in 1936. Two years later it was decommissioned from use and donated to Colorado Springs for city beautification. The engine stood in a Colorado Springs park, unused for over eighty years. The Cumbres & Toltec arranged to "borrow" the engine, raise a half-million dollars for its repair, and get it back into service on their rail line. A team of about four skilled engineers spent thousands of hours restoring the engine. It's now the oldest working locomotive in the United States.

"This is the authentic West," said John Bush. "Here the past is not forgotten. Hell, it isn't even past."

Beginning with *The Good Guys and the Bad Guys* in 1969, Westerns arrived at the C&TSRR in droves. The train made an appearance in a Gene Hackman Western about endurance horse racing called *Bite the Bullet*. It also showed up in *Wyatt Earp*, *The Legend of*

HOW TO GET THERE

500 South Terrace Avenue
Chama, NM 87520
888-286-2737
cumbrestoltec.com

WHERE TO STAY

Chama Station Inn
423 Terrace Avenue
Chama, NM 87520
575-756-2315
chamastationinn.com

WHERE TO EAT

Foster's Hotel Bar Restaurant
393 Terrace Ave, Chama, NM 87520
Chama, NM 87520
575-756-2296
Fosters1881.com

the Lone Ranger, and *Butch & Sundance: The Early Days*. Seth McFarlane visited the C&TSRR with his spoof of Westerns, *A Million Ways to Die in the West*.

In a rare non-Western, Steven Spielberg and George Lucas used the train for the opening sequence of *Indiana Jones and the Last Crusade*. The flashback, which features a young River Phoenix, follows Indiana Jones as he escapes a swashbuckling crew of artifact thieves. Jones jumps onto a train carrying circus animals and comes face-to-face with a lion and a train car filled with snakes. Along the way, Jones picks up a fear of a snakes, an admiration for whips, and a small scar under his chin.

The C&TSRR runs more than one hundred freight cars and twenty-one passenger cars for 129 days in a row, from Memorial Day into October. Half-day and full-day trips are available on tourist or coach-class cars. The C&TSRR also offers parlor car and deluxe options.

SELECTED FILMOGRAPHY

Spielberg, Steven, dir. *Indiana Jones and The Last Crusade*. USA: Paramount Pictures, 1989.

20

TRUCHAS AND THE HIGH ROAD TO TAOS

Robert Redford used this town along the scenic High Road to Taos in his adaptation of John Nichols's The Milagro Beanfield War.

Situated on the scenic High Road to Taos, the small town of Truchas made a memorable appearance in Robert Redford's adaptation of *The Milagro Beanfield War*. Written by Taos local John Nichols, the novel explores class struggles and the fight for water in a fictional New Mexico community.

Filled with mysticism, culture and backstories, it was a difficult book to convert to film. Nichols summarized the novel with characteristic bluntness: "[The book,] like anyone who has ever tried to explain New Mexico to an outsider, tends to ramble. Like our state, the novel is big, it is bold, and it is mostly empty spaces," wrote Nichols. Nonetheless, Redford made an overture at the adaptation.

Nichols later wrote about the experience of working on this adaptation in his book, *Dancing on the Stones: Selected Essays*. "I've had my teeth bashed out playing hockey, and I spent nine years protesting the Vietnam War. I've been married and divorced three times, and I raised two children. I've been in a head-on collision, and I almost died of endocarditis two years ago. I then went through five years of congestive heart failure that culminated in open-heart surgery. But I can safely say that the toughest thing I ever did in my life was to have a movie made of my third novel, *The Milagro Beanfield War*," Nichols wrote in "Night of the Living Beanfield: How an Unsuccessful Cult Novel Became an Unsuccessful Cult Film in Only Fourteen Years, Eleven Nervous Breakdowns and $20 Million."

Christopher Walken walks through Truchas in *The Milagro Beanfield War* (1988). Courtesy of Universal Pictures.

Nichols wasn't the only one who struggled during the shoot. The production budget doubled during filming. Initially set for 9 million dollars, the costs ballooned to $20 million because weather delays and small complications added up over time. For instance, the crew attempted to create a beanfield using real stalks only to have them freeze every night, requiring that they be replaced the next day—over and over again. Nichols joked that the little film transformed into an expensive epic.

Redford and the ensemble cast made local and national news, in part because of their fame and, in part, because of infamy. Redford cast a diverse group, but few were of the same Hispanic heritage as the characters in the book, and a minor controversy followed as a result. Rumors also swirled that Redford was in a romantic relationship with one of the actors in the film.

All the same, the film was completed and released in 1988 to mostly middling reviews. A few critics praised the lofty goals of the movie while others were unenthused by the ensemble cast and the subtle points about class warfare. In the years since its release, the film has garnered something of a cult status and promoted Truchas as a destination.

Interestingly, Truchas wasn't Redford's first choice for shooting. He hoped to use nearby Chimayó, which is both picturesque and closer to Santa Fe. Chimayó holds a chapel known as a sacred Catholic site, and it gets heavy religious traffic. The city turned down the production. Fortunately for Truchas, the traditionally Hispanic enclave made an appropriate setting for a fictional town in desperate need of water. Truchas was itself formed as the result of Spanish land grants and is still governed by regulations that date back to those times.

Truchas is surrounded by beautiful views of the Sangre de Cristo Mountain Range. The little town is best visited as a single stop along the High Road to Taos. (The "Low Road to Taos" is also scenic, complete with views of the Rio Grande.) The High Road goes through a number of dramatic viewpoints and passes many art galleries. Allow several hours for the drive.

Officially, the scenic byway begins in Santa Fe and heads north toward Española. Start on US Route 84/285 out of Santa Fe and continue through Pojoaque until the intersection with New Mexico State Road 503. Take a right on New Mexico State Road 503 toward Chimayó.

Chimayó has several claims to fame aside from turning down Robert Redford. Predominantly it is known as a sanctuary site, with soil that reputedly heals believers. Every year, tens of thousands of faithful Catholics make a long pilgrimage to the Santuario on foot. Some people travel as far as one hundred miles this way, although the site is also reachable by automobile. The Santuario de Chimayó (15 Santuario Drive, Chimayó, NM, 87522; 505-351-9961, holychimayo.us) draws several hundred-thousand visitors per year. Allow time to walk around the grounds and traditional Spanish gardens if you visit.

From Chimayó, take New Mexico State Road 503 to New Mexico State Road 76, through a ghostly landscape of rolling hills that

HOW TO GET THERE

Truchas can be reached along the High Road to Taos, New Mexico State Road 76.

WHERE TO STAY

Hilton Santa Fe Buffalo Thunder
20 Buffalo Thunder Trail
Santa Fe, NM 87506
505-455-5555 4
hiltonbuffalothunder.com

One of the stars of the comic book adaptation *2 Guns* stayed at this casino resort to make use of the attached golf course during shooting. Another comic book adaptation, *Scalped*, shot several scenes for its pilot episode in the lower-level casino floor. The pilot was not picked up to series and is not available to watch.

WHERE TO EAT

Rancho de Chimayó
300 Juan Medina Road
Chimayó, NM 87522
505-351-4444
ranchodechimayo.com

winds its way to Truchas. All along the road are local craftspeople and artist galleries. A number of weavers cluster around Chimayó—look for Ortega's Weaving Shop (53 Plaza Del Cerro, NM, 87522; 505-351-4215, ortegasweaving.com)—and several sculptors have galleries farther up the High Road—look for Oviedo Carvings & Bronze (New Mexico State Road 76, Chimayó, NM, 87522; 505-351-2280, oviedoart.com).

The High Road bends sharply as it goes through Truchas, and it's easy to miss the funky hamlet, so keep your eyes open. Truchas is filled with art galleries and is home to the historic Our Lady of the Rosary Mission Church, built in 1764.

From Truchas, the road makes its way to Las Trampas Historic District and the San José de Gracia Church, which are National Landmarks and are overseen by the park service. The church and parts of the surrounding village are remnants of an eighteenth-century Spanish village and survive as a distinct community today.

The High Road then passes through Picuris Pueblo (Pueblo View State Road 75, Peñasco, NM, 87553; 575-587-2519, picurispueblo.org), known for its efforts to return bison to tribal lands, and the road edges close to Sipapu Ski & Summer Resort (5224 New Mexico State Road 518, Vadito, NM, 87579; 800-587-2240, sipapu.ski). Although one of the smaller ski zones in the area, Sipapu has a good hill for starting skiers.

Eventually, the High Road reaches Rancho de Taos, just a few miles north of the byway's terminus in Taos itself.

SELECTED FILMOGRAPHY

Redford, Robert, dir. *The Milagro Beanfield War*. USA: Universal Pictures, 1988. Film.

Peter Fonda and Dennis Hopper arrive at Taos Pueblo in *Easy Rider*, © 1969 (renewed 1997) by Columbia Pictures Industries, Inc. All Rights Reserved. Courtesy of Columbia Pictures.

21

TAOS PUEBLO

Peter Fonda and Dennis Hopper buzzed past the Pueblo in Easy Rider.

Along with Acoma, one of the oldest continuously inhabited villages in North America, Taos Pueblo is on the United Nations Educational, Scientific and Cultural Organization (UNESCO) World Heritage List and famed for its multi-story adobe architecture and picturesque, mountainous backdrop.

Taos played a pivotal role in the Pueblo Revolt that excised the Spanish in 1680. Later, the Pueblo residents spearheaded another rebellion against Territorial Governor Charles Bent in 1847. The people at Taos were tough and rebellious and steadfast. Hard to imagine a better setting for one of the hallmark films of the countercultural 1960s.

Dennis Hopper and Peter Fonda's *Easy Rider* went through a number of early renditions and its origins are a bit hazy. The script might have been born of the experience of real motorcycle gangs. Or, perhaps it was a purely fictional screenplay. Over the years, Fonda and Hopper were not always consistent in describing the genesis of the film. Most retellings agree that Fonda called Hopper one day with the germ of an idea about a motorcycle film. Fonda was confident that such a film could be successful because he had done well previously with *The Wild Angels*. Hopper would later say that he and Fonda wrote just about every word in the script, but Terry Southern, who received a writing credit, also claimed much of the responsibility.

At the time, the concept was an odd one. Ne'er-do-wells crossing the country with money from a recent drug score did not fit with the general film aesthetic of the 1960s. There also was not much of a precedent for guerrilla films succeeding at the box office. Additionally, Hopper wanted to challenge conventions by infusing the film with European and Indian influences. "I was interested in trying to make the first American art film and outside the studio system," said Hopper years later.

The risk in the film wasn't necessarily in the story, though. The risk was with first-time director and character actor Hopper. For years, Hopper appeared in smaller parts as a villain or eccentric townsperson. He had a brief appearance in Clint Eastwood's *Hang 'Em High* (see location 42 for more on that film). At the time it wasn't clear that Hopper could handle his directing or acting tasks in the film.

Easy Rider struggled before production even began. Actor Rip Torn butted heads with Hopper at a dinner meeting, and for years Hopper maintained that Torn pulled a knife on him. Torn, for his part, claimed that Hopper was the one who acted threateningly. They settled the matter in court more than twenty years later. At the time, though, Hopper and Fonda were forced to look at alternatives and ultimately hire a relative unknown for the part. Jack Nicholson went on to receive an Academy Award nomination for his role as an alcoholic lawyer in the film.

In an interview, Hopper would later say that he came upon Taos by accident when he and his production manager took a wrong turn. "So he got the directions wrong and I ended up in Taos . . .

in the plaza and this Indian guy came up to me as I was getting out of the car and said, 'The mountain is smiling on you, I know where you need to go.' He took me out to New Buffalo, which is what I was looking for. . . . I was looking for a commune. So, that's the way it started." (The New Buffalo commune, perhaps the most famous of its kind in New Mexico, was not available for filming. The crew built a facsimile in California.)

HOW TO GET THERE

Taos Pueblo Tourism
120 Veterans Highway
Taos, NM 87571
575-758-1028
taospueblo.com

WHERE TO STAY

El Monte Sagrado
317 Kit Carson Road
Taos, NM 87571
575-758-3502
elmontesagrado.com

WHERE TO EAT

Michael's Kitchen
304-C North Pueblo Road
Taos, NM 87571
575-758-4178
michaelskitchen.com

The film premiered at the Cannes Film Festival where Hopper and his work took France by storm. *Easy Rider* received the First Filmmaker Award, and Hopper captured the European imagination with his flamboyant attire. The film's momentum continued when it was released in the United States later in the year.

Produced for less than a million dollars, *Easy Rider* became the third-highest-grossing film of 1969, raking in some 40 million dollars in the United States alone. *Easy Rider* set a standard for inexpensive, independent filmmaking. It also became an iconic reference point for the back-to-the-land hippies that were flourishing at the time. The movie's values became so associated with New Mexico that numerous additional communes were founded in the proximity of the New Buffalo.

In the process of making the film, Hopper fell in love with the

Taos area. He returned after *Easy Rider* and purchased a home that once belonged to Mabel Dodge Lujan. One of the prominent figures in Taos history, Lujan hosted salons and acted as a patron for the Taos Society of Artists. Hopper, doubtlessly attracted by the artistic history of Taos, lived in the area on and off for at least fifteen years. Other members of his family moved to Taos permanently.

The complex at the heart of Taos Pueblo is open to the public and every bit as picturesque as it was when Hopper captured it in *Easy Rider*. Guided tours leave from the visitor's center every twenty or thirty minutes depending on the season. Pueblo residents, some of whom live in the historic structure, sell art and food around the Pueblo.

SELECTED FILMOGRAPHY

Hopper, Dennis, and Peter Fonda, dirs. *Easy Rider*. USA: Columbia Pictures, 1969. Film.

22

RIO GRANDE GORGE BRIDGE

One of the highest bridges of its kind, the distinctive Rio Grande Gorge Bridge appeared in Terminator Salvation.

In *Terminator Salvation*, the fourth film in director James Cameron's android saga, a mysterious survivor with a violent past finds himself on the run with two teenage rebels. The trio survives attacks by a massive robot and a motorcycle-like android only to find themselves trapped on a bridge by two aerial drones. The drones open fire then grab the two youngest members of the three-person party and toss them in a holding pen. The bridge crumbles and gives way to the Rio Grande far below.

Completed in 1965, the bridge is among the highest in the United States, standing 650 feet above the flowing Rio Grande river. About a quarter of mile long, the bridge is open to car and foot traffic. On windy days, the walk can be a bit harrowing, but there is a walkway. There's a parking lot on the southwestern end of the bridge for those willing to try crossing on foot.

With its signature arches and dramatic view of the river, the Rio Grande Gorge Bridge has become a staple of New Mexican filmmaking. The bridge is easy to reach and provides dramatic photography for sci-fi films, road-trip flicks, and whodunits. For *Natural Born Killers* the crew shot a wedding scene on one of the lookouts atop the bridge. Oliver Stone later recalled it as one of the strangest weddings he'd ever seen.

Terminator Salvation was the most expensive film made in New Mexico when shot. With a reported budget of around $200 million, the film sported an all-star cast and a flashy lineage. To dress their vision of a world almost destroyed by sentient machines, the

A Hunter-Killer ship fires at the heroes of *Terminator Salvation* (2009) as they drive across the Rio Grande Gorge Bridge. Courtesy of Warner Bros.

crew placed wrecked cars along the roadsides and on the bridge. The production took over the roadway for several days as they dressed it for the *Terminator* world. They shot some of the bridge-chase action practically, without CGI, filming a high-speed drive across the bridge with stunt actors hanging from the back of a wrecker truck.

This battle scene in *Terminator Salvation* turns into an aerial dogfight over the Rio Grande as human-piloted jets take on aerial android drones. The sequence ends when actor Sam Worthington, playing Marcus Wright, falls into the river. Perhaps the most beautiful stretch of river in the state, the Rio Grande above Taos is a big seasonal draw.

The Rio Grande between the bridge and Alcalde downstream is a premier destination for water sports. When the cubic feet per second run high, usually during the runoff season in spring and summer, the Rio Grande fills with whitewater rafters in inflatable

HOW TO GET THERE

From Taos, take New Mexico State Road 522 north for approximately 3.5 miles to the last four-way intersection of town. Turn left to get onto US Route 64 West. Travel about 8 miles. Cross the bridge, and the parking area is on the left.

WHERE TO STAY

Hotel Luna Mystica
25 ABC Mesa Road
El Prado, NM 87529
575-613-1411
hotellunamystica.com

This collection of restored trailers has a lot of ambiance and relaxed charm.

WHERE TO EAT

Taos Mesa Brewing
20 ABC Mesa Road
El Prado, NM 87529
575-758-1900 ext. 1
taosmesabrewing.com

Dubbed the "Mothership," this spacious brewery hosts a regular series of concerts and events.

boats. The stretch of the river directly below the bridge is usually called the Taos Box and is known for fast-moving rapids that require more technical boating ability. Farther downstream, the racecourse is often filled with touring companies that put novices on boats and take them down the river. A number of outfitters offer excursions that usually stage around Pilar. Alternatively, when the river moves slower, boaters can rent stand-up paddleboards and inflatable kayaks.

The river, the gorge, and much of the surrounding land to the north of the Bridge are all part of the Rio Grande Del Norte National Monument (1120 Cerro Road, Cerro, NM, 87519; 575-758-8851). The monument includes over 240,000 acres of managed wilderness, hiking trails, and developed camping. The popular West Rim Trail covers about nine miles of the monument and starts at the parking area at the end of the bridge.

SELECTED FILMOGRAPHY

Stone, Oliver, dir. *Natural Born Killers*. USA: Warner Bros., 1994. Film.

McG, dir. *Terminator Salvation*. USA: Warner Bros., 2009. Film.

23

RIO CHAMA AND ABIQUIÚ DAM & LAKE

Unspoiled views of red rock cliffs make this area perfect for Westerns.

A high desert sprinkled with mountains, New Mexico has few perennial bodies of water. The Rio Grande is probably the most famous of the bunch, but the Rio Chama—and the Abiquiú Dam above it—are ideal for period films thanks to views unspoiled by modern developments.

A tributary of the Rio Grande, the Rio Chama is one of the most picturesque rivers in the Southwest. It winds its way among sandstone cliffs, high plains, and forests. Twenty-four miles of the river were designated as wild and scenic in 1988 and zoned against development. In keeping with that designation, much of the Chama is difficult to reach.

Just below the Abiquiú Dam, the Chama has a fairly consistent water flow and few traces of modernity. This part of the river is one of the few that are easy to reach on mostly paved roads and is therefore convenient for Westerns. *Sweetwater*, *Hostiles*, *Jane Got a Gun*, *Comanche Moon*, and the remake of *The Magnificent Seven* all shot scenes here.

In one of the more unique film-support services, New Wave Rafting Company (2110 New Mexico State Road 68, Embudo, NM, 87531; 800-984-1444, newwaverafting.com) often brings rafting guides to a shoot and stands by with boats and emergency equipment as cast and stunt actors make their way across the river. They also shuttle camera equipment across the waterway as needed.

The Chama is a popular destination for multiday floats. Experienced boaters can enter a lottery with the Bureau of Land

Daniel Craig and Olivia Wilde crawl out of Abiquiú Lake in *Cowboys & Aliens* (2011). Courtesy of Universal Pictures.

Management to obtain a permit. Permits are limited to reduce traffic and human impact on the landscape. Several local river-guide companies also offer boating and camping expeditions down the river, including New Wave. The trips take about three days and include hot springs, dinosaur tracks, class II or III rapids, and unspoiled views of nature. The trip encompasses a "totally different landscape and geology than the rest of the state," said Britt Huggins, owner of New Wave Rafting Company. "It's a whole different world, something out of Utah."

HOW TO GET THERE

Take US Route 84/285 to New Mexico State Road 96 and then go left on County Road 162, down past the picnic areas for the Rio Chama location. For the lake, stay on New Mexico State Road 96 or go back to US Route 84/285 and head north to the lake exit.

WHERE TO STAY

In addition to camping at the Abiquiú Dam & Lake, lodging is available at Ghost Ranch and in the town of Abiquiú (see locations 23 and 24).

Just above the most popular film site on the Rio Chama, the Abiquiú Dam & Lake also draws productions. The lake is visible in *Cowboys & Aliens*. Chased by an alien space cruiser, Daniel Craig, playing Jake Lonergan, and Olivia Wilde as Ella Swenson crash into the Abiquiú Lake. Afterward they swim to shore for a brief romantic moment before a big alien interrupts them. To shoot the scene, director Jon Favreau stood on a stand-up paddleboard to watch the action. During breaks, he said later, the crew jumped into the reservoir to cool off. Favreau called it his favorite day of the shoot.

The Abiquiú Dam & Lake offer boating, picnicking, and camping. The lake also has great views of the surrounding red rock formations.

Daniel Stern, Billy Crystal, and Bruno Kirby in *City Slickers* (1991). Courtesy of Columbia Pictures.

24

GHOST RANCH

The inspiration for many of Georgia O'Keeffe's paintings, Ghost Ranch is also frequently used for Westerns. Billy Crystal and friends tripped through the sandstone canyons in the Western send-up City Slickers.

The sandstone formation and cliffs at Ghost Ranch have inspired paintings, photos, and films for years. But no artist is as closely associated with the area as Georgia O'Keeffe. She made prevalent use of the topography in some of her best-known works.

History at Ghost Ranch, though, extends much farther into the past. Paleontological evidence places dinosaurs in the area some 200 million years ago. Specifically, the Ghost Ranch area was home to the Coelophysis bauri, a small predator with a long snout. Some of the best examples of the species were excavated at Ghost Ranch during a series of paleontological efforts.

Standing water and plentiful game drew Native peoples to the area about a thousand years ago, and in the nineteenth century the area became a hideout for cattle rustlers. The homestead was built decades later and dubbed Rancho de Los Brujos, "the Ranch of the Witches," due to occupation by purported ruthless thieves and killers. Reportedly, many who went into the area never returned, and

Ronald Colman in *The Light That Failed* (1939). Courtesy of the Paul Andrew Hutton Collection and Paramount Pictures.

ghost stories and ghoulish tales arose about the place. The name took hold. Later, as the tales spread and the property changed hands to English-speaking families, the name was warped into the shorter, but equally descriptive, Ghost Ranch.

The area became a working dude ranch in the 1930s. The Presbyterian church acquired the property in 1955 and transformed the ranch into a conference center. Today, the venue hosts several hundred conventions a year and a slew of educational and spiritual talks. It is also open for day visitors and hiking.

The Light That Failed used Ghost Ranch as a substitute for Africa in an adaptation of a Rudyard Kipling novel. Released in 1939, the film starred Ronald Colman as a British soldier and Walter Huston as a journalist. Colman attempts to paint his masterpiece as he loses his vision. This was the second filmed adaptation of that novel.

The source material for the film *City Slickers* was far less auspicious. While sifting through romantic comedy scripts—hot off the success of *When Harry Met Sally*—Billy Crystal happened to catch television programming about a new vacation trend in the United States in which tourists paid to take part in real-life cattle drives. The seed for *City Slickers* was sown. He ran with the idea and, acting as executive producer, hired screenwriters and a director.

Crystal also took the starring role as a middle-aged New Yorker in desperate need of a change. His friends buy him tickets to a cattle drive, and the mock adventure rapidly turns into a real crisis. "I wanted to make *Deliverance* with laughs," Crystal told *Entertainment Weekly*. "There's more of me in *City Slickers* than anything else I've ever done. I created and tapered the character to something I could plug all my talents into. . . . I hope to become the first of the Jewish Western action heroes."

The production team built a modern ranch set near the entrance to Ghost Ranch. The cast learned to ride horses, rope steer, and generally conduct themselves like cowboys. Two hundred head of cattle were brought into the Ghost Ranch area so that the film would look authentic. A cabin from the set is still standing and visible on the drive into Ghost Ranch. The area has remained popular with filmmakers. *City Slickers* director Ron Underwood, for instance, returned there in 1993 with *Speechless*, a rom-com about two political speechwriters starring Geena Davis and Michael Keaton.

Ghost Ranch is open for visitation for a small fee. The grounds have two museums, one that covers human history and another that features paleontology, including the famed Coelophysis. In the summer the pool is open for an additional fee. There's also plenty of hiking trails near the center of the ranch.

During busy periods, Ghost Ranch operates their own cafeteria, which is open to guests. On occasion, film crews use the rustic dining hall, which has a distinctly summer camp–style vibe.

HOW TO GET THERE

280 Private Drive 1708
Abiquiú, NM, 87510
(Off U.S. Route 84)
505-685-1000
ghostranch.org

WHERE TO STAY AND EAT

Ghost Ranch offers rustic lodging that includes breakfast in their dining hall. Lunch and dinner are available in the dining hall as well for a fee.

CREW MEMORY

I will never forget the long days, sandy hair, sunburnt skin, grimy fingernails. Working on a movie is not always as glamorous as you may think, but after a long day of hard work, nothing gets better than looking up into the distance and seeing what beautiful landscape you get to work with. Ghost Ranch is one of those locations that make your mouth drop and your eyes open wide. I will never forget the film day when for over twelve hours back riders all dressed in black leather trailed back and forth down the bright-red canyon all day, establishing one of the most beautiful shots I have ever seen. Field days at Ghost Ranch are the best days, not to mention the cotton candy–colored sunset. —*Anonymous*

SELECTED FILMOGRAPHY

Underwood, Ron, dir. *City Slickers*. USA: Columbia Pictures, 1991. Film.

Wellman, William, dir. *The Light that Failed*. USA: Paramount Pictures, 1939. Film.

25

LAS VEGAS

Dozens of early Westerns starring Tom Mix featured Las Vegas. More recently, the Coen Brothers crafted a thrilling chase scene in No Country for Old Men *on the Las Vegas streets.*

1984's Cold War fever nightmare *Red Dawn* opens with an insert shot of a statue of Teddy Roosevelt and his "Rough Riders." Famous for charging up San Juan Hill during the Spanish American War, the Rough Riders were used as a symbol of American resilience against incredible odds by the filmmaker John Milius. Perhaps, ironically, a number of the real Rough Riders hailed from Las Vegas, where Milius shot the film. Had Milius chosen to use Las Vegas as itself, instead of fictional Calumet, Colorado, he could hardly have found a town more representative of the American West and the American dream. Las Vegas has alternately been a railroad boomtown, a film-production center, and a lawless frontier town.

Founded in 1835 on land-grant parcels, Las Vegas grew rapidly when the railroad arrived in 1879. The train brought commerce, and the city capitalized, becoming one of the busiest rail stops in the Southwest. To accommodate the many travelers on the rail, the railroad and private investors constructed several large hotels. Three of these hotels are still standing and feature prominently in films.

The Fred Harvey Company, famous for its buttoned-up hospitality across the American West, built the Castañeda Hotel not far from the tracks in 1898. The building was disused after a few decades but had a prominent role as the operations base for invading

Russian soldiers in front of a tank in *Red Dawn* (1984). Courtesy of the Paul Andrew Hutton Collection and MGM/UA.

Charlie Sheen, C. Thomas Howell, and Patrick Swayze on the Las Vegas streets in *Red Dawn* (1984). Courtesy of the Paul Andrew Hutton Collection and MGM/UA.

Still from Romaine Fielding's *The Rattlesnake* (1913).
Courtesy of the City of Las Vegas Museum.

communist forces in *Red Dawn*. The Hotel was recently restored and is currently open for guests.

The Atchison, Topeka and Santa Fe Railroad constructed their own hotel in Las Vegas in 1886. The ninety-thousand-square-foot stone Montezuma Castle is still standing, although it is no longer in use as a hotel. The castle was purchased by the Armand Hammer Foundation in 1982 and transformed into the Armand Hammer United World College of the American West (UWC-USA) (New Mexico Route 65, Montezuma, NM, 87731; 505-454-4200, uwc-usa.org; tours are available intermittently—please check for scheduling). Coincidentally, Hammer's great-grandson, Armie, would star in Disney's *The Lone Ranger*, which shot in New Mexico in 2012. The massive building appeared as a haunted house in the off-color horror film *The Evil* in 1978. Actor Richard Crenna starred as a psychologist who attempts to rehab the old mansion only to discover that the building is haunted.

The Plaza Hotel, built in 1882, has an even more prominent role in film. In the earliest days of moviemaking in Las Vegas, director Romaine Fielding commandeered the entire building and renamed it "Hotel Romaine" while he and his crew stayed there in 1913. The paint from Fielding's signage was still visible a century later when the Coen Brothers used the Plaza for one of the most exciting shootout sequences in *No Country for Old Men*.

Before arriving in Las Vegas, Fielding enjoyed a meteoric rise in the burgeoning film industry. Within a few years, Fielding went from a stage actor to running the Southwest division of Philadelphia-based Lubin Films. He picked up directing, writing, and producing on-the-go while setting up his shooting company in Tucson, Arizona, and then Silver City, New Mexico. While in Southern New Mexico, Fielding got word of picturesque Las Vegas and decided to have a look. Las Vegas had it all, and Fielding made it his production base. He housed his crew in the Plaza and made a handful of silent films, most notably *The Rattlesnake*. His company also shot the ambitious five-reeler *The Golden God* while staying there. The film purportedly used five thousand background actors and included a lengthy battle scene with realistic explosions. The prints of the film were later destroyed in a fire.

Early Western star Tom Mix succeeded Fielding in Las Vegas. Born in Oklahoma, Mix knew how to ride horses and had a knack for on-screen tricks. Mix was an expert rider and did most of his own stunts. He was also a marksman, reportedly able to shoot the buttons off a blouse. Not one to shy away from his own legends, Mix didn't deny rumors that he fought with Roosevelt's Rough Riders and in the Boxer Rebellion, even though he had not.

The tall tales only added to his fame. At the height of his popularity in the 1920s, Mix earned twenty thousand dollars per week and starred in hundreds of short, silent films. Mix came to Las Vegas as part of a greater Southwestern swing for the Selig Polyscope Company and took advantage of the town's enduring Western character. Mix made several dozen films in Las Vegas, using the same studio space that Fielding had used several years earlier.

Much of the character that made Las Vegas appealing a century ago still exists. At present, the town has more than nine hundred structures on the National Historic Registry. Because of those many antique buildings, Las Vegas has a uniquely "Main Street" look that has helped the town reemerge as a great destination for filmmaking and tourism. The sci-fi comedy *Paul*, which starred Seth Rogen as a slacker alien escaping the government, filmed several key sequences in the Las Vegas historic district.

The chase scene in *No Country for Old Men* shot in the historic district as well. Josh Brolin, playing Vietnam Veteran Llewellyn Moss, limps his way through the excitement, in part because he had a real-life injury. He told *New York Magazine* that "Two days after I got the movie, I was on my motorcycle and a car cut me off. I said that I had a hairline fracture on my collarbone, but it was completely snapped in half. When we started the movie, I couldn't even lift the gun. The only reason I was able to do the movie is

HOW TO GET THERE

From Interstate 25, take exit 343 toward New Mexico State Road 283. Turn left onto New Mexico Avenue and then right onto West National Avenue. Turn left on North Gonzales Street and left again on Plaza Street

WHERE TO STAY

Plaza Hotel
230 Plaza Street
Las Vegas, NM 87701
505-425-3591
plazahotellvnm.com

Castañeda Hotel
524 Railroad Avenue
Las Vegas, NM 87701
505-425-3591
castanedahotel.org

Union rules mandate that film crew members working more than thirty miles from their home offices must be provided with housing. As they did a century ago, many crew members still stay at the Plaza Hotel, although tales of ghosts dissuade some.

WHERE TO EAT

Dick's
705 Douglas Avenue
Las Vegas, NM 87701
505-425-8261
dickspubandrestaurant.com

because [my character] Llewelyn gets shot in the right shoulder at the beginning of the story. I wore a sling the whole time when I wasn't working."

Start by visiting the Plaza Hotel and then make a loop around the plaza itself and turn onto Bridge Street. Many of the buildings in this area date from the nineteenth century and have been preserved and, in some cases, restored.

SELECTED FILMOGRAPHY

Coen Brothers, dir. *No Country for Old Men*. USA: Miramax, 2007. Film.

Fielding, Romaine, dir. *The Rattlesnake*. USA: Lubin Manufacturing, Co. 1913. Film.

Milius, John, dir. *Red Dawn*. USA: MGM/UA Entertainment Company, 1984. Film.

Mix, Tom, dir. *Local Color*. USA: Selig Polyscope, 1915. Film.

Mottola, Greg, dir. *Paul*. USA: Universal Pictures, 2011. Film.

Trikonis, Gus, dir. *The Evil*. USA: New World Pictures, 1978. Film.

26

FARMINGTON

This industrial town at the crossing of three rivers is close to geologic landmarks including Shiprock and the Bisti Badlands.

Early in director Oliver Stone's über-violent social commentary *Natural Born Killers*, a tacky news-magazine show reenacts the journey of the rebellious lovers at the heart of the movie. When pulled over by a police officer, one of the replica outlaws yells, "How the hell you get to Farmington?"

In preparation for the killing-spree road-trip flick, Stone scouted much of the Southwest. Famed for making dark and conspiratorial features, Stone worked from a script by Quentin Tarantino for *Natural Born Killers* and found Farmington ideal for a number of scenes. Memorably, Farmington's most famous nearby landmark, Shiprock, on Navajo Nation land, appears in the background in a dream sequence. The nearby "Devil's Highway" was originally numbered 666 and then later renamed US Route 491, and it is used for some traveling shots.

When released in 1994, the film descended into controversy. Critics found the stylized violence to be "too much." Their fears came to fruition when several real-life copycat criminals reportedly patterned murders after scenes in the film. Stone, though, said that the film rubbed people in the press wrong because the story was largely an indictment of the tabloid era in media production.

Farmington itself is less controversial. The area, with its three passing rivers, was popular first with Ancestral Pueblo people and then successive groups of Navajo, Jicarilla Apache, and Ute

Shiprock as it appears *The Lone Ranger* (2013). Courtesy of Disney.

peoples. When American settlers arrived in the area, they farmed apples at first. But in the mid-twentieth century oil production supplanted farming, and Farmington continues to be a busy provider of fossil fuels.

The most visible point of interest near Farmington is the formation known as Shiprock. Rising six hundred meters out of the desert floor, Shiprock is the remnant of a massive volcanic eruption that happened about 30 million years ago. All that remains of the volcano is a solidified channel of lava with dikes, or walls of lava, emanating from the core. Rather accurately, the Navajo people call the formation the "Winged Rock."

Like the structures in nearby Monument Valley, Shiprock is an unmistakable geographic feature that makes for a dramatic backdrop. The lone mountain appeared in the World War II drama *Sundown* in 1941. It became a staple of Western films starting with *My Darling Clementine* just five years later. John Ford's take on the shootout at the OK Corral, which actually happened in Tombstone, Arizona, used Shiprock briefly. And some majestic shots of it appear in *The Lone Ranger* (2013), the second version of the classic Western hero's tale to shoot in New Mexico. The comedic Western *A Million Ways to Die in the West* also features Shiprock in the background.

In the sci-fi film *Finch*, Tom Hanks wanders past Shiprock in desperate need of water while succumbing to the desert heat. The film is directed by *Game of Thrones* standout Miguel Sapochnik and focuses on a man teaching a robot the meaning of life in a post-apocalyptic world.

As it is a sacred place to the Dine (Navajo) people, Shiprock is protected and not open for off-roading, hiking, or climbing. There are a number of great views of the mountain from several of the roads around Farmington, however, including US Route 491.

Another unforgettable geographic landmark near Farmington, the Bisti Badlands, is among the stranger geographic segments of New Mexico. Otherworldly, Bisti looks like a replica of an alien world but is actually the heavily eroded remnants of Cretaceous

Period sediment. The wilderness area is filled with funky rock formations like hoodoos, mushrooms, and arches made from multicolored, crumbling shales. In fact, the Navajo people named the area "Bisti" (among sandstone) and "De-Na-Zin" (crane).

The remote area is probably best known as the source of an impressive fossil dubbed the "Bisti Beast." A member of the tyrannosaur family, the beast is actually part of a new genus and named after the badlands. The bones of the massive predator were excavated in 1997 and put on display at the New Mexico Museum of Natural History in Albuquerque.

The badlands may look like a set, but they've only featured in a few productions. They make a brief appearance in the 1977 cult thriller *Sorcerer*, which was supposed to be a big-budget coup for director William Friedkin, who was riding high on the success of *The Exorcist*. Contrary to the title, the film is not about a mystical being. The title is actually a reference to a big-rig truck. Even so, the end of the film is a surreal dream sequence with aerial footage of the badlands. The badlands had a more generic appearance in *Stargate: Universe* as an alien world on the other side of a space portal. The television crew for *Stargate* spent four days shooting in the remote desert.

The badlands are remote, have no facilities, and are exposed in the summer. There are also no maintained trails. The best access to the wilderness area is off New Mexico State Road 371. After mile marker 70, head east on County Road 7297 for three miles to the parking area.

Farmington makes a convenient base to explore a handful of impressive archaeological attractions nearby; most notable are the Chaco Culture National Historical Park (1808 County Road 7950, Nageezi, NM, 87037; 505-786-7014, nps.gov/chcu), Aztec Ruins National Monument (725 Ruins Road, Aztec, NM, 87410; 505-334-6174 x0, nps.gov/azru), and the Salmon Ruins (6131 US State Road 64, Bloomfield, NM, 87413; 505-632-2013, salmonruins.com). Chaco is roughly an hour and a half south of Farmington, but the drive is well worth it for anyone who has even a passing interest in Native American history. The castle-like structures are remnants from the apex of Ancestral Puebloan culture. The Aztec Ruins National Monument is not as expansive, and it was built years later, but it is an impressive example of Pueblo architecture as well. For an earlier period of Puebloan history, Salmon Ruins are among the first to be extensively excavated in the region.

In addition to Bisti, Shiprock, and the historic sites, Farmington is also close to Navajo Lake State Park (36 Road 4110 #1, Navajo Dam, NM, 87419; 505-632-2278, www.emnrd.state.nm.us/spd/navajolakestatepark.html). The second-largest lake in New Mexico, it is a good destination for boating, fishing, and camping.

HOW TO GET THERE

The Farmington area is adjacent to several small airports. It's also an easy four-hour drive from Albuquerque up US Route 550.

WHERE TO STAY

Farmington has several chain motels and hotels.

WHERE TO EAT

Three Rivers Brewery
101 East Main Street
Farmington, NM 87401
505-324-2187
threeriversbrewery.com

Three Rivers is a cavernous restaurant, brewery, and distillery built in a historic structure. The venue is also packed with bar games. The cast on *Jumanji: The Next Level* hung out at the pub frequently during the several weeks they shot at Shiprock.

CREW MEMORY

My first gig in the film industry was as a producer's assistant for one of Tom Hanks' s movies filming in New Mexico. I have been a resident of New Mexico for eleven years but was still excited to travel within the state as there was so much to see. One location we were blessed to use for a production site was Shiprock. The local Natives there, the Navajo, fed us breakfast each morning for the three days we were there. I was told by one of the locals that they call it Winged Rock because of a legend that has to do with a great bird bringing the Navajo to their present land. I never looked at the beautiful Shiprock the same after that. There was something magical about the place. It was hard to explain, but just knowing how sacred that land was made things more interesting. The Navajo gave us permission to film there, but there were areas we were not allowed to disturb with any driving or walking.

We were there at the end of March, and it was so cold that I just couldn't stay warm. I had three hand warmers in each pocket of my coat and foot warmers under my feet in my boots, and I still could not stay warm. I think on our last day of shooting Shiprock itself hinted that we overstayed our welcome. First, we had a nasty dust storm, and it didn't matter how covered we were. The dust found its way inside our coats and goggles. It was so windy and dusty that we were all bundled up and could barely tell each other apart. Once that subsided, it started to snow and continued until there was thin layer of snow covering the ground. The snow was not bad, but it did drop the temperature even more.

When the snow subsided, it started to rain, and it was pouring down! We had to run for cover as the dirt was turning into thick clay. Most film-industry veterans were equipped with shoe covers so that their boots or shoes would not have to endure the sticky mud. I was not so lucky. I put my boots in a bag as the mud was so thick I needed a knife to scrape it off. I had other shoes in my car, but they were not sturdy enough for cold weather.

After the rain subsided it started to hail. "Really??" I said out loud while I was in my car starting to get warm. I was just tired of the drastic changes in weather and was ready for a nap.

—Laura DiMauro, Producer's Assistant

CREW MEMORY

When *Stargate* was prepping to shoot at White Sands, I presented Bisti to the director. The show runner saw the photos and came back the next season to shoot his episode at Bisti.
—*Sam Tischler, Unit Production Manager*

SELECTED FILMOGRAPHY

Cooper, Robert C., and Brad Wright, creators. *Stargate Universe*. Season 2, episode 8, "Malice." USA: SyFy, 2010. TV series.

Friedkin, William, dir. *Sorcerer*. USA: Universal Pictures, 1977. Film.

McFarlane, Seth, dir. *A Million Ways to Die in the West*. USA: Universal Pictures, 2014. Film

Stone, Oliver, dir. *Natural Born Killers*. USA: Warner Bros., 1994. Film.

Verbinski, Gore, dir. *The Lone Ranger*. USA: Walt Disney Pictures, 2013. Film.

PART IV

ALBUQUERQUE AREA

Kirk Douglas greets a visitor to the set of *Lonely are the Brave* (1962).
Courtesy of the Paul Andrew Hutton Collection and Universal Pictures.

27

SANDIA MOUNTAINS

In the tragic conclusion of Lonely Are the Brave, *Kirk Douglas finds himself trapped in the jagged mountains east of Albuquerque with the police hot on his trail. Douglas's lost cowboy character dies as a sorrowful avatar for the disappearing West.*

Pursued by the police, Kirk Douglas's cowboy hero in *Lonely Are the Brave* flees toward the mountains on horseback. He hopes to draw cover under the boulders and trees and maybe stay alive long enough to escape. The odds, though, are against him. Walter Matthau, as the local sheriff, hovers overhead in a chopper while police on the ground are catching up. Douglas does all he can to hide in the wilderness of the Sandia Mountains.

Lonely Are the Brave was based on *The Brave Cowboy* by Edward Abbey and adapted by screenwriter Dalton Trumbo. A sort of bard of the desert Southwest, Abbey would eventually be best known for his eco-terrorist novel *The Monkeywrench Gang*, about a group of misfits who plan to destroy a dam in order to save the environment. Trumbo, for his part, was a blacklisted screenwriter who served time for not complying with the House Un-American Activities Committee and then wrote in secret for years. Trumbo received multiple Academy Awards, some under his own name and others under the pseudonyms he used while blacklisted.

The resultant combination of Trumbo and Abbey's liberal, nonconformist voices became an ode to rugged individualism and an elegy for the dying West. Douglas plays a wanderer named John W. Burns who cuts fences to move around the plains in accordance with changing property boundaries and cattle-grazing areas. He only goes into civilization to visit a friend and, once in town, is bombarded with trouble. Burns gets in a bar fight, becomes the target of a sheriff's ire, and sets off a massive manhunt when he runs from the law.

Much of the chase sequence for this manhunt was shot in the low-lying western foothills of the Sandia Mountains. In the years since the film was made, large swathes of this area have been developed into sprawling homes, making the landscape the living embodiment of Abbey and Trumbo's elegy. Just as Douglas plays a character on the border between encroaching modernity and untouched wilderness, the heavily forested Sandias stand on the border between Albuquerque's urban sprawl and the mountains.

In an interesting game of six degrees of separation, Trumbo was the subject of a self-titled film that starred Bryan Cranston in 2015, and Cranston is best known for playing Walter White in the hit television series *Breaking Bad*, which shot in Albuquerque and the Sandia Mountains as well. For the iconic penultimate episode of *Breaking Bad*, titled "Granite State," the crew built a cabin (since removed) at the base of a small cliff off the north side of Ellis Trail #202, off New Mexico State Road 536. In the episode, Walter White is smuggled inside of a propane tanker truck to a hiding spot at an isolated cabin in New Hampshire. He waits there, possibly for his resurgent cancer to kill him, while a national manhunt for him has begun.

Spanish for "watermelon," the Sandias are a southern extension of the Rockies and rise ten thousand feet out of the high desert floor. Much of it is managed by the United States Forest Service, although the City of Albuquerque owns and operates an assortment of trails and picnic areas. Elena Gallegos Open Space (7100 Tramway Boulevard NE, Albuquerque, NM, 87122; 505-768-5353, cabq.gov/parksandrecreation/open-space/lands/elena-gallegos-open-space), for instance, features covered picnic areas, grills, and access to the Pino Trail, all maintained by the City of Albuquerque. The mountain is a popular escape for Burqueños hoping to cool off, go for a hike, or just take in the views.

The Sandias are best known as the home of the Sandia Peak Tramway (30 Tramway Road NE, Albuquerque, NM, 87122; 505-856-1532, sandiapeak.com). The tram is one of the longest of its kind in the world, stretching for almost three miles from Tramway Road to the summit. Built largely by helicopter in 1966 to support access to the ski slopes on the other side of the mountain, the tram is supported by just two large towers strong enough to support the aerial span. In winter, skiers can take the tramway to the backside of the Sandia Peak Ski Area. In summer, hikers enjoy the view from the tram before embarking on short walks around the top of the mountains. The ride on the tram passes near, or over, the same terrain featured in *Lonely Are the Brave*.

Perhaps the most popular hike in Albuquerque covers much of the same ground. La Luz Trail goes straight up the Sandias for about seven miles starting at a Forest Service parking area in the foothills. Rocky and often covered with snow, this trail is not for the faint of heart, but it is rewarding for those able to muscle up the three thousand feet in elevation change. Park one car at the trailhead and another at the tram, hike up the mountain to the station near the summit, and ride the tram back down. Or, take the tram down and hike the connecting path two miles back to the trailhead.

The mountains are also accessible by road on the eastern flank. From Interstate 40, the Turquoise Trail loops through Tijeras and goes north toward Madrid. The small town of Cedar Crest is

HOW TO GET THERE

By tram, take Interstate 40 to Tramway Boulevard northbound. Take Tramway Boulevard all the way to Tramway Road, then hang a right into the tram base.

By freeway, continue on Interstate 40 East to the exit for New Mexico State Road 14.

WHERE TO STAY

Sandia Resort & Casino
30 Rainbow Road
Albuquerque, NM 87113
505-796-7500
sandiacasino.com

Owned by Sandia Pueblo, the Resort & Casino host some notable annual events like the National Fiery Foods and Barbecue Show.

WHERE TO EAT

Greenside Cafe
12165 New Mexico State Road 14
Cedar Crest, NM 87008
505-286-2684
greenside.cafe

a good place to stop along this route. It's home to an independent grocery store that occasionally allows filming called the Triangle Grocery (12545 New Mexico State Road 14, Cedar Crest, NM, 87008; 505-281-3030, trianglegrocery.com). There's also a small museum of archaeology and material culture (22 Calvary Road, Cedar Crest, NM, 87008; 505-281-2005) that is worth taking a look at.

After the turn off State Road 14 to the Sandias, the Tinkertown Museum (121 Sandia Crest Road, Sandia Park, NM, 87047; 505-281-5233, tinkertown.com) is one of the quirkiest spots in the state. Built seemingly ad hoc, the museum is filled with mechanized dioramas composed of handmade figurines. The museum also has a collection of random American paraphernalia and a boat that once circled the globe.

Another oddity deep in the mountains, Sandia Man Cave (the trailhead of the .47 mile hike is off of New Mexico State Road 165, and the parking lot is marked with a sign) is purportedly the site of prehistoric inhabitation. The discovery of the cave changed academic perceptions of the human migration into what is now North America. Later research indicated that some of these artifacts appear to have been manipulated in a lab, and the integrity of the find has since been called into question.

The road to the top of the Sandias features a number of other hiking trails and additional access to the Ski Area. Snowfall is inconsistent, but the Ski Area usually manages to be open at least part of each winter. The area has thirty-five runs and three lifts. New Mexico State Road 536 ends in a loop and a parking area at the Sandia Crest with access to a scenic viewpoint and a gift shop.

SELECTED FILMOGRAPHY

Miller, David, dir. *Lonely Are the Brave*. USA: Universal Studios, 1962. Film.

Central Avenue in *Breaking Bad* (2008–2013).
Courtesy of Sony Pictures Entertainment.

28

BREAKING BAD AND *BETTER CALL SAUL* IN ALBUQUERQUE

In 2004, screenwriter Vince Gilligan called his friend and fellow writer Thomas Schnauz to commiserate about their respective job searches. Both writers had major credits at the time, but Hollywood is never easy, and they were concerned about the future. "We were talking on the phone bemoaning our unemployment, he mentioned an article he had read in the *New York Times* in which some guy had put a meth lab in the back of an RV and was driving around and cooking meth like some sort of demented ice cream truck driver, I suppose," said Gilligan in a later interview. "It seems to me, in hindsight, a terrible idea for a TV show."

Gilligan set the pilot in and around Riverside, California, in part because he had done some research in the area. Not all that far from Los Angeles, Gilligan also knew that he could make it home from Riverside every night and could sleep in his own bed. Television studios, however, are loathe to miss out on rebate opportunities, and Sony dispatched producer Karen Moore to New Mexico, where a relatively new incentive program beckoned. "So,

I flew in. It was bitterly cold. A location scout that I had contacted took me out to this red rock area in this little [Native American] town called To'hajiilee. And I was like, 'Oh my god. This is incredible.' So, I go back to the hotel, I call Vince, and I said, 'This place is fantastic,'" said Moore.

Gilligan, flexible and aware of budgetary constraints, came around to Albuquerque quickly. "The look of Albuquerque, with the amazing endless skies with the big, puffy cumulus clouds and the Sandia Mountains to the east, just the geography of the area, the landscape was so cinematic that it actually changed my thinking and changed the way we shot the show," he said.

Locally, the pilot script worked its way to the Albuquerque Film Office, part of the city's economic-development program, where Ann Lerner gave it a read. Lerner, film liaison for the city, recognized that the script could be controversial, but it could also be a big break for the city. She presented the story to Mayor Martin Chavez, who wasn't bothered by the show's exploration of drugs and criminality.

Others around town, however, were troubled by the fact that the show billed itself as a methamphetamines story. The produc-

The Dog House as it appears in *Breaking Bad* (2008–2013). Courtesy of Sony Pictures Entertainment.

Bryan Cranston as Walter White takes a call in Albuquerque's Civic Plaza in *Breaking Bad* (2008–2013). Courtesy of Sony Pictures Entertainment.

tion had trouble renting space and even getting access to parking lots in Albuquerque. Initially, it was tough for the production to find locations.

Worse yet, it took some convincing to get the network onboard with such a risky pilot. At the time, AMC was rebranding itself on the strength of *Mad Men*. They were not convinced that they wanted a second show, much less one about a middle-aged cancer victim who goes from "Mr. Chips to Scarface." Even with all these reservations, they green-lit the series.

It took a few years, but thanks in part to the birth of Netflix, *Breaking Bad* found an audience. The show became a phenomenon in its final three seasons and changed the landscape of television while claiming landmarks in Albuquerque and rebranding the "Land of Enchantment."

Over five seasons of *Breaking Bad* and six for the spin-off *Better Call Saul*, the franchise has filmed all over the state—in some of its most picturesque landscapes and some of its darkest corners. This chapter focuses on accessible Albuquerque locations.

One of the most popular and frequently visited locations may be Walter White's home, which is featured in every season of the show. The home is private, and the owners, growing weary of enthusiasts throwing pizzas onto the roof above their garage (see the episode entitled "Caballo Sin Nombre" in season three), asked to be left alone. They also built a fence surrounding much of the house to limit visibility. We won't list the physical address here.

Several of the signature restaurants featured in the show are much easier to visit. The most famous of the bunch has to be the Dog House (1216 Central Avenue NW, Albuquerque, NM, 87102; 505-243-1019), a hot dog stand where Aaron Paul's Jesse Pinkman wheels and deals. In a more desperate encounter, Walter White meets with wife Lydia at the Grove Cafe & Market (600 Central Avenue SE, Suite A, Albuquerque, NM, 87102; 505-248-9800, thegrovecafemarket.com) to ask for one last chance. Mike Ehrmantrout, the enforcer of the series, routinely dines at Loyola's Family Restaurant (4500 Central Avenue SE, Albuquerque, NM, 87108; 505-268-6478, loyolasfamilyrestaurant.com).

No eatery is as central to the story, however, as the Twisters location in the South Valley (4275 Isleta Blvd SW, Albuquerque, NM, 87105; 505-877-2727, mytwisters.com/isleta). The local fast-food spot is the site of some of the most pivotal moments in both series. The restaurant, of course, is known as Los Pollos Hermanos in the show and is the front business for drug kingpin Gustavo Fring. The dining area is filled with *Breaking Bad* artwork.

Fring laundered money and moved drugs through his restaurant, but White owned a car wash. That car wash is in operation and open to the public. Now part of a chain called Mister Car Wash (9516 Snow Heights Circle NE Albuquerque, NM, 87112; 505-298-8833, mistercarwash.com/location/snow-heights), the waiting area includes a shrine to the show, complete with a signed photo of the location's personnel who worked on the show. As you look at the displays and watch your car get cleaned, you may recognize the spot in the pilot where White lost consciousness and set off the events of the show.

Visible from Interstate 25 and easy to access off Central Avenue, the Crossroads Motel (1001 Central Avenue NE, Albuquerque, NM, 87106; 505-242-2757), with its distinctive multicolored walkways and windows, is worth driving past. The motel appears frequently in the show as the "Crystal Palace," a flophouse for the meth addicted in the show.

Better Call Saul used the restaurant on the first floor of the Hyatt Regency Albuquerque, Forque Kitchen and Bar (330 Tijeras Avenue NW, Albuquerque, NM, 87102; 505-842-1234, hyatt.com/en-US/hotel/new-mexico/hyatt-regency-albuquerque/albuq/dining), for a number of memorable scenes. It is the setting for the title character's tequila-inspired grift, for instance. Bob Odenkirk, playing Jimmy McGill, convinces a local blowhard to pay for top-shelf drinks here. And Jimmy and his partner, Kim, succeed in a ruse at the bar for laughs and free drinks.

Across the street from the Hyatt, the Bernalillo County Annex (415 Tijeras Avenue NW, Albuquerque, NM, 87102) provided a great space for some of the court scenes at the end of season three, which were shot in an out-of-use courtroom on the third floor.

Erin Moriarty in downtown Albuquerque in *Blood Father* (2014).
Courtesy of Lionsgate Premiere.

29

DOWNTOWN ALBUQUERQUE

Scores of films and televisions shows have used Central Avenue as a substitute for other urban centers.

Downtown Albuquerque sits at several physical and cultural intersections. The area sprang up at the crossroads between historic communities at Old Town, Martineztown, and Barelas. Old Town, once the center of Spanish colonial activity in what is now Albuquerque, had roots in the beginning of the eighteenth century.

The Atchison, Topeka and Santa Fe Railroad carved a path through the Rio Grande Valley in areas that were largely devoid of floods. The railroad also decided to use Albuquerque as a waypoint station for vehicular repair and for railroad offices. (For additional details, please see the entry on the Rail Yards.) When completed in 1880, the railroad changed the dynamic of the fledgling city altogether.

To accommodate the new business and its many employees, enterprising locals organized the area around the railroad into quadrants and quickly built housing. Warehouses for shipping the region's goods followed shortly afterward. Soon, Central Avenue was born, and the footprint of modern-day downtown was all but established. Fire-resistant brick buildings arose en masse at the turn of the century as investors in the busy area wanted safer, more permanent structures.

The introduction of Route 66 beginning in 1927 reorganized the downtown area and made the automobile the new center of commercial activity. Car dealers and tourist shops popped up along Central Avenue, as did the hallmark KiMo Theater. The design of the theater artfully blends an Art Deco aesthetic with the Pueblo Revival, creating a style often called "Pueblo Deco," which is unique to the area.

Central Avenue between the Alvarado train station and the roundabout at 8th St. NW is frequently used in films and television. The area provides an urban tableau that can mimic other cities in the United States. At the very least, downtown has subbed in for Chicago, Illinois; Santa Monica, California; and Las Vegas, Nevada. Downtown is by far the easiest place to catch a glimpse of a film crew at work. In active film environments, at least one or two productions will use downtown almost every week. Look for closed roads and signs declaring "Special Event."

The S. H. Kress Building (416 Central Avenue SW, Albuquerque, NM, 87102), now a historic landmark, was built as a department store in 1925. It appears in the Kevin Costner film *Swing Vote*. At press time, the building is not occupied, but it was a functional retail storefront and open to the public until recently.

The distinctive Occidental Life Building (301 Gold Avenue SW, Albuquerque, NM, 87102), built in 1917 and inspired by the Palazzo Ducale in Venice, Italy, pops up in a films like *Marvel Studios' The Avengers* and *Transcendence*. It's a private office complex, but the unique façade is visible from the street.

Another architectural highlight of the corridor is the Old Post Office (123 4th Street SW, Albuquerque, NM, 87102), which is also on the National Register of Historic Places. Now a charter high school, the building is over a century old. It appeared in the USA Network international thriller *Dig*.

Downtown is a dependable destination for drinks, food, and concerts. In addition to the KiMo, the Sunshine Theater, and the El Rey are both historic venues with a busy lineup of concerts and touring acts. The nearby Albuquerque Convention Center (401 2nd

Street NW, Albuquerque, NM, 87102; 505-768-4575, albuquerquecc.com) also hosts talks and concerts on a regular basis. In front of the Convention Center, the Civic Plaza has an unmistakable metal awning that features in *Breaking Bad* and *Gamer*, among other productions.

HOW TO GET THERE

Central Avenue corridor between Broadway Boulevard NE and 8th St. NW.

WHERE TO STAY

Hotel Parq Central
806 Central Avenue SE
Albuquerque, NM 87102
505-242-0040
hotelparqcentral.com

A remodeled mental hospital, the Parq Central is another production staple.

WHERE TO EAT

Farina Pizzeria & Wine Bar Downtown
510 Central Avenue SE
Albuquerque, NM 87102
505-243-0130
farinapizzeria.com

CREW MEMORY

Marisol Adler was one of the regular directors for a series called *The Night Shift*, which filmed here in New Mexico from 2014 through 2017. Whenever we'd go on a location scout, our first stop would always be Zendo Coffee, on 2nd Street just south of Lead. Marisol would happily buy us whatever we'd like, to go, and then we'd have delicious coffee for the scout.

Sometimes going to Zendo first wouldn't be convenient—for instance, if the location scout were in the other direction. But she and the crew usually found a way to schedule all the different location visits in such a way that the coffee shop wouldn't be too far from our first stop.

It was a great ritual that helped bond the crew and made us feel appreciated. Thanks, Marisol! —*Ted Slampyak, Storyboard Artist (storytellersworkshop.com)*

CREW MEMORY

I'll never forget walking onto the set of a movie starring Tom Hanks. They turned an entire block in the business district of downtown Albuquerque into a post-apocalyptic scene full of sand and destroyed vehicles. It was eerily realistic. THEN. The twenty-foot tall earthmover truck arrived. . . . It was AMAZING. I had never seen a Komatsu truck on city streets before, much less one being driven by Tom Hanks. That was one amazing set to have in New Mexico! —*Dominique Mazire, Director's Assistant*

CREW MEMORY

It was the middle of the night, the roads were barricaded off, the tension was hot, it was going to be a long evening. The big chase was in the works for the evening; this shot was going to be pure action and excitement. I will never forget the night I had a lock up on Gold Street. Finally, the clock hit 2:00 a.m., and the crew was ready to shoot the big shot; everyone with warm coffee in hand had been preparing for this moment all week. The hero vehicle was all ready to go, the camera mounted, the stuntmen geared up. Suddenly, the director calls "action," and they got JUST what they were looking for, plus more. That night the crew got their chase scene, but they also got an unexpected flat tire and a window explosion. Luckily, the crew had insurance. Downtown scenes have so many variables, but luckily Albuquerque has the best police force to block off streets so that people stay safe and the production gets just the shots they are looking for! —*Anonymous*

SELECTED FILMOGRAPHY

Kring, Tim, and Gideon Raff, creators. *Dig*. USA: USA Network, 2014. Television series.

Stern, Joshua Michael, dir. *Swing Vote*. USA: Touchstone Pictures, 2008. Film.

30

ALBUQUERQUE LIKE A FILM LOCAL

With more than a dozen stage spaces, plenty of offices, and plenty of urban practical locations, Albuquerque is far and away the busiest filming destination in New Mexico. It's also the biggest city in the state. Roughly half of New Mexico's population resides in the metropolitan area, including most of the state's crew base. Although it is growing rapidly, Albuquerque is still a small town at heart, and it's not difficult to bump into film crew at any of their usual cafes, restaurants, and entertainment locations.

Long days on sets require copious amounts of caffeine. Most of the time, the craft-services department provides coffee to the crew, but people escape to gourmet coffee shops as often as their schedules allow. In the downtown area, Zendo (413 2nd Street SW, Albuquerque, NM, 87102; 505-926-1636, zendocoffee.com) serves artisanal lattes in an artistic space. Humble (4200 Lomas Boulevard NE, Albuquerque, NM, 87110; 505-289-9909, humblecoffeeco.com) has two locations, and both have reliably excellent brews. Cutbow (1208 Rio Grande Boulevard NW, Albuquerque, NM, 87104; 505-355-5563, cutbowcoffee.com) roasts their own beans.

The catering department prepares meals while on set, but when they are off set, members of the crew have a stable rotation of restaurants they patronize. Vinaigrette (1828 Central Avenue SW, Albuquerque, NM, 87104; 505-842-5507, vinaigretteonline.com) has locations in Albuquerque and Santa Fe. They serve fresh salads and sandwiches that satisfy the most health-conscious eaters. Flying Star Cafe (3416 Central Avenue SE, Albuquerque, NM, 87106; 505-255-6633, flyingstarcafe.com) is something of an Albuquerque institution and is a good spot for elevated diner food and for doing homework. Favorites for international food include Taj Mahal (1430 Carlisle Boulevard NE, Albuquerque, NM, 87110; 505-255-1994, tajmahalabq.com) and Fan Tang (3523 Central Avenue NE,

Albuquerque, NM, 87106; 505- 266-3566, fan-tang.com). For local cuisine, the Frontier Restaurant (2400 Central Avenue SE, Albuquerque, NM, 87106; 505-266-0550, frontierrestaurant.com) is a wacky, short-order Albuquerque mainstay. Its fresh tortillas are legendary, and the green chile stew will make most New Mexicans very happy.

For more upscale eats, Campo at Los Poblanos (4803 Rio Grande Boulevard NW, Los Ranchos de Albuquerque, NM, 87107; 505-338-1615, lospoblanos.com/dining) is a perennial choice for farm-to-table creations. Reservations are recommended, and diners should try to arrive early so they have time to visit the farm shop for organic lavender products to take home as souvenirs. Two food halls recently opened in Albuquerque, and both offer a wide selection of local and international cuisine in a trendy setting. The Sawmill Market (1909 Bellamah Ave NW, Albuquerque, NM, 87104, 505-563-4473, sawmillmarket.com) opened in 2020 in a remodeled lumber yard that was later used as special effects and construction shop for multiple productions. 505 Central Hall (505 Central Ave NW, Albuquerque, NM, 87102, 505central.com) is located right downtown.

Albuquerque has fostered a micro-brew movement for over a decade and is home to a number of quaffable brews. The flagship Marble Brewery (111 Marble Avenue NW, Albuquerque, NM, 87102; 505-243-2739, marblebrewery.com) has expansive outdoor seating and live music. Bow & Arrow Brewing Co. (608 McKnight Avenue NW, Albuquerque, NM, 87102; 505-247-9800, bowandarrowbrewing.com) might have the best designed space of any of the breweries, with a sleekly Southwestern interior.

A handful of distillers and mixologists recently joined the brewers around town. Still Spirits (120 Marble Avenue NW, Albuquerque, NM, 87102; 505-750-3138), across the street from Marble Brewery, offers a selection of elevated mixed drinks if that's more your speed. Broken Trail Brewery and Distillery (6902 Menaul Boulevard NE, Albuquerque, NM, 87110; 505-221-6281, brokentrailspirits.com) creates their own vodka and other liquors for drinking.

The Central Avenue corridor in downtown is the hub of Albuquerque's nightlife and draws a constant influx of college students and partiers along with the film-crew set. Try Anodyne (409 Central

Avenue NW, Albuquerque, NM, 87102; 505-244-1820) for billiards, arcade games, and a rustic vibe. Sister Bar (407 Central Avenue NW, Albuquerque, NM, 87102; 505-242-4900, sisterthebar.com) has dancing and good late-night eats.

Apart from chain movie theaters and the historic KiMo (see the "New Mexico Theaters" chapter), Albuquerque has the high-brow Guild Cinema (3405 Central Avenue NE, Albuquerque, NM, 87106; 505-255-1848, guildcinema.com), which features arthouse fare and hosts private events. Performance venues include Popejoy Hall on the University of New Mexico campus (at the corner of Redondo Drive NE and Cornell Drive SE, Albuquerque, NM, 87106; 505-277-9771, popejoypresents.com) and the National Hispanic Cultural Center (1701 4th Street SW, Albuquerque, NM, 87102; 505-246-2261, nhccnm.org).

Live-music spots cluster around the downtown corridor, some in historic buildings. The Sunshine Theater (120 Central Avenue SW, Albuquerque, NM, 87102; 505-764-0249,sunshinetheaterlive.com) and the Historic El Rey Theater (622 Central Avenue SW, Albuquerque, NM, 87102; 505-510-2582, elreylive.com) draw big acts.

Although erratic weather is the bane of all filmmakers in New Mexico, Albuquerque has a preponderance of sunny days, so outdoor activities are a big draw for locals and visitors. The Sandia Mountains, which border Albuquerque to the east, have a number of trails for those who don't mind elevation and steeper trails (see location 27). For shadier, less strenuous activity there's a trail that follows the Rio Grande through the middle of the Paseo del Bosque (translated as the "Forrest Walk").

If you need to buy gifts, try Page 1 Books (5850 Eubank Boulevard NE, Suite B-41, Albuquerque, NM, 87111; 505-294-2026, page1book.com), Bookworks (4022 Rio Grande Boulevard NW, Albuquerque, NM, 87107; 505-344-8139, bkwrks.com), or Palms Trading Company (1504 Lomas Boulevard NW, Albuquerque, NM, 87104; 505-247-8504, palmstrading.com). Old Town is full of stores to buy fun, local gifts, but in particular it is home to the Candy Lady (424 San Felipe Street NW, Albuquerque, NM, 87104; 505-243-6239, thecandylady.com), which is infamous for its blue rock candy.

The Albuquerque Rail Yards. Photo by Amanda Lynn Robinson.

31

ALBUQUERQUE RAIL YARDS

This majestic remnant of Albuquerque's train days is now the most versatile filming location in the state.

Built for the Atchison, Topeka & Santa Fe Railroad beginning in 1914, the more than twenty-five massive brick buildings at the Rail Yards served as repair shops for steam engine locomotives. The complex includes a rail car turntable, a blacksmith shop, a machine shop, a fire house, and other service edifices needed for the business. Inside, workers cleaned boilers and painted and fabricated trains. At their busiest, these plants repaired forty locomotives a month. The shops fueled the local economy and employed people who lived in the surrounding Barelas neighborhood. The Rail Yards remained in service as repair facilities into the 1990s.

Following their closure, the City of Albuquerque faced a difficult choice. The Rail Yards would be incredibly expensive to convert into modern usage, but they are historically significant and visually appealing. Another remnant of the railroad era, the Alvarado

Hotel, was torn down when business dwindled in the area, and Burqueños still regret the loss. The experience left a bad taste in their mouths, so they were loath to let the Rail Yards fall to a similar fate. Hence the solution was raised to put the Rail Yards to work as a film studio.

The City of Albuquerque arranged to jointly operate the all-but-abandoned Rail Yards with Q Studios (see the "New Mexico Studios" chapter for more details). Since then, the buildings have appeared in scores of films and television shows. At press time, plans are ongoing to transform the Rail Yards into the "Film Production Center of Excellence" for Central New Mexico Community College. The junior college would use the Rail Yards as a studio and a classroom space. Those plans will require a significant investment, and despite interest from the city they are not guaranteed to succeed. For the time being, the Rail Yards remain a temporary studio and event space.

Thanks to the sheer size of the structures, film crews can use the interiors as fully functional studios by rigging green screens and constructing full-scale sets. Meanwhile, the exteriors, with their decorous windows and brick facades, can be transformed to resemble urban locations or futuristic wastelands. With a little bit of ingenuity, the warehouses can stand in for almost anything. As a result, the Rail Yards could be the most in-demand location in Albuquerque.

Marvel Studios transformed part of one cavernous building into a New York City viaduct for the spectacular battle scene at the end of *Marvel Studios' The Avengers*. Captain America, the Black Widow, Iron Man, Thor, and Hawkeye convene to discuss their strategy here as an evil hoard of aliens pours into Manhattan. The crew built a full-scale replica section of New York City near Grand Central Terminal inside the Rail Yards. The footage of the battle moves seamlessly from real photography of New York City to moments filmed in Albuquerque.

Perhaps even more creatively, Marvel transformed the exterior of the Rail Yards garage into a block of Kolkata, India. The com-

The Albuquerque Rail Yards. Photo by Amanda Lynn Robinson.

pleted scene served as an introduction to Bruce Banner / the Hulk, played by Mark Ruffalo. They built enough of Kolkata that the scene is set up with a "long shot" of a young girl who leads the audience through the city and to Banner. The crew returned to the Rail Yards for another Hulk scene, where the Hulk crashes to earth all but naked, leaving a huge impact crater that the crew was able to build inside one of the warehouses. Harry Dean Stanton has a short cameo in the scene as a security guard who banters with Banner.

The Rail Yards can be viewed from the outside via a short drive south from downtown Albuquerque. For a better look, the Rail Yards is open to the public for farmer's markets once a week from May through October (10:00 a.m.–2:00 p.m. on Sundays, railyards market.org). Typically, the market uses some of the interior space as well as the courtyard. The December holiday market uses the Rail Yards in a similar way and draws a huge crowd each year.

Another way to get a closer look is to visit the Wheels Museum (1100 2nd Street SW, Albuquerque, NM, 87102; 505-243-6269, wheelsmuseum.org), which celebrates the railroading history of the area along with other methods of transportation. Inside the building at the southern end of the Rail Yards is an eclectic collection of antique automobiles, model train sets, railroad equipment, and a scale model of the now-demolished Alvarado Hotel.

CREW MEMORY

This location goes way back for me. I remember the first time seeing it when my *padrino*, Armando Trujillo, took my sister and me on a drive past the old Rail Yards when I was in elementary school. The massive gentle beasts of buildings looked so majestic and almost happy—invitingly greeting and welcoming their visiting guests. We never entered the property, but as we creeped past in his old blue Dodge, I remember him telling us about how this place was bustling and full of energy, fixing old trains and a big part of the community. That location holds truth about what it was and still is—a part of the community. In college, I was given the opportunity to participate in a photo shoot inside the Rail Yard property. My sister was one of my models, and I remember her wearing outfits that I made and posing with our two pet ferrets inside the large repair shop. The photo even made its way into the *Daily Lobo*. I was lucky to have visited it twice in my studies. Looking back, it was a magnificent experience, and I'm thankful that I got to see the old sheet-metal building before it burned down. Even back then, our wonderful hosts made remarks of how the "movie industry" never cleaned the windows they dirtied while filming a movie in there. This year, 2020, I stepped onto the property again, and when I asked about the local lore of the place, our guide informed us that there was a story of a buried train on the property. After they scanned the area with ground-penetrating radar they found evidence of something large and metal buried on the southwest side of the once-movable platform between the two large workshops. No one really knows exactly what it is, why it's there, or when it was put there. —*Amanda Lynn Robinson, Set Designer*

CREW MEMORY

I was a freshman at UNM and my sister, who was a senior in the School of Architecture, had reached out to me saying she needed help with a project. The assignment was to construct clothing out of everyday materials, so my sister, Amanda, asked me to model some old curtains for her. After everything was fitted, trimmed, and sized, photos needed to be taken of me in the dress, so we made our way to the Rail Yards. The end result was perfect. The recycled dress combined with the old rustic building was nothing short of art on all platforms. The photo ended up making the front page of the *Daily Lobo*, paired with an article about the school project. That was the first time I really appreciated the Albuquerque Rail Yards. It's not too good of a setting for anyone or anything. It is for all mediums of art and expression.

HOW TO GET THERE

777 1st Street SW
Albuquerque, NM 87102

The entrance to the Rail Yards will likely be marked for traffic control during events.

WHERE TO STAY

Hotel Andaluz Albuquerque
125 2nd Street NW
Albuquerque, NM 87102
505-242-9090
hotelandaluz.com

The Andaluz often hosts actors, producers, and visiting studio execs. New Mexico–born Conrad Hilton, of the Hilton hotels empire, built the hotel in 1939, and it went through several owners before it was restored in 2008.

The Spanish Revival lobby has been featured in several productions including the USA Network series *Briarpatch*. The show is based on an Edgar Award–winning novel of the same name by Tom Ross, which was adapted for television by Andy Greenwald and stars Rosario Dawson.

WHERE TO EAT

Brixens
400 Central Avenue SW
Albuquerque, NM 87102
505-242-2400
brixens.com

The first time I shot "professionally" at the Albuquerque Rail Yards was on season 1 of Netflix's *Daybreak*. Being on set is intimidating enough as it is, but to see the Rail Yards transformed made me truly realize how timeless this structure was. It had been transformed into an enormous abandoned cereal factory, complete with scaffolding and other dressing that went along with it, and to see it on the big screen was incredible. —*Alyssa Robinson, Assistant Prop Master*

SELECTED FILMOGRAPHY

Neveldine, Mark, and Brian Taylor, dirs. *Gamer*. USA: Lionsgate, Lakeshore Entertainment, 2009.

Whedon, Joss, dir. *Marvel Studios' The Avengers*. USA: Paramount Pictures, 2012.

PART V

CENTRAL NEW MEXICO

Silent films gave Mary Pickford her start.
Courtesy of Wikimedia Commons.

32

ISLETA PUEBLO

The first New Mexico film was shot at this Pueblo, just south of Albuquerque, in 1897.

Over a span of fifteen years, three of the most iconic names in American filmmaking visited and shot at Isleta Pueblo. The first was in 1897, when the Edison Manufacturing Company made the motion picture *Indian Day School.*

Employees at Thomas Edison's Orange Labs in New Jersey began to experiment with motion picture technology in 1889. Their inspiration for the device likely arrived with photographer Edward Muybridge, who created the zoopraxiscope, a primitive motion-picture projector. Muybridge wanted to partner with Edison on a motion picture device that worked like a phonograph. Edison was taken with the idea, if not with Muybridge himself, and assigned his inventors to the project. The mechanics of a phonograph did not translate to visual mediums, though. Instead, the lab found success using rolls of celluloid passed along sprockets. Their recording device was called the kinetograph. The short loops of film it produced were to be viewed on a device called the kinetoscope. The first kinetoscope parlors, where patrons could put coins in the machine then peer into the viewer and watch the motion pictures, opened in 1894.

Employees of the Edison Manufacturing Company, one of the many divisions of Thomas Edison's umbrella behemoth, captured footage of incredible human activities for the kinetoscope. One short showed a couple kissing, for instance. One captured a dancer with a flowing dress. In another, a bodybuilder flexed his muscles. A few of these "actualities" show Native American tradition. The Sioux Ghost Dance and their Buffalo Dance were both shot at the Black Maria Studio at Edison's lab. The studio was named for its paddy wagon–like appearance. It also had a roof that could be raised to allow in sunlight.

The introduction of portable kinetographs made it possible for filming to move outside of the studio. Meanwhile, the large format of projectors brought additional detail to moving pictures, and on-location footage was soon in demand. The Edison Manufacturing Company realized that they could delight audiences with scenes of daily life. They also discovered that they could partner with tourism promoters for even more extraordinary footage.

New Mexico made for a great destination. After the railroad arrived in the territory in 1878, a push for tourism stoked the American imagination with tales of lost civilizations and exotic Native customs. Isleta Pueblo, emblematic of a romanticized Native culture, was easy to reach from Albuquerque and "exotic" enough to entice Edison.

Established around 1300, Isleta Pueblo is a Tiwa-speaking village of about three thousand people. Thanks to its proximity to the Rio Grande, its land is relatively fertile and excellent for farming. Much of this fertility comes from the occasions when the Rio Grande would flood, and the village appeared to float in the overflow waters. For this reason, the Spanish dubbed it Isleta, meaning "small island." Isleta was a booming village when the Edison Manufacturing Company visited with their kinetographs.

It's unlikely that Edison himself traveled to New Mexico, but his technicians made the trip to Isleta and set up their kinetograph on a stationary mount to record students, most of them younger than ten, emerging after class. This film strip has been digitized by the Library of Congress as part of its database on recorded American history (it can be viewed online at loc.gov/item/00564534).

By the time the Edison Manufacturing Company shot *Indian Day School*, William Kennedy Dickson, who was a former employee and part of Edison's original kinetograph team, had already formed the rival Biograph Company in New York City. Dickson and his partners built a studio similar to the Black Maria and made primarily actualities until 1903, when narratives gained traction. Then-unknown David Llewylyn Wark (D. W.) Griffith moved from Louisville, Kentucky, at just the right time, therefore, with his hope of selling his writing to the Biograph Company. Instead of being hired as a writer, Griffith fell in as an actor for the company. He moved up the ranks quickly, however, to direct *The Adventures of Dollie* in 1908, launching a career that changed the medium.

After only a few years at Biograph in New York, Griffith traveled to Los Angeles to make the first film shot in Hollywood. Over the following years he directed *The Birth of a Nation* and *Intolerance*, essentially inventing feature-length, narrative films.

In 1912, Griffith and blossoming star Mary Pickford arrived in Albuquerque to make a short Native American fantasy film. Pickford was one of the idols of the silent-film era and captured the country's imagination when she married fellow actor Douglas Fairbanks. In *A Pueblo Legend*, Pickford played a Hopi woman who falls in love with the local War Chief and goes in search of a sacred stone. At the time, residents of Isleta were so offended by the film's bastardization of their culture that they briefly detained Griffith in an attempt to stop the film from being made. Ultimately the Pueblo released him, however, and the filming was finished.

Indian Day School (1898). Courtesy of the Library of Congress.

Fittingly, Isleta Pueblo was used in *House Made of Dawn* six decades later. The film, based on N. Scott Momaday's novel of the same name, is about reclaiming Native American identity. What better place to shoot such a tale, than on the same spot where Native culture was appropriated for early filmmaking.

The Pueblo is home to the second-oldest mission church in the state. Originally built in 1613, Mission San Agustin de Isleta (71 Tribal Rd. 35, Isleta Pueblo, NM, 87022; 505-869-3398, www.nps.gov/subjects/travelspanishmissions/mission-san-agustin-de-isleta.htm) was rebuilt in 1710. Made from adobe brick and painted all in white, it is a classic example of Spanish Colonial architecture. The church is still at the center of the plaza and is an active site of Catholic worship.

HOW TO GET THERE

Take Interstate 25 South to New Mexico State Road 314 / Isleta Boulevard and go south to Tribal Road 42.

WHERE TO STAY

Isleta Resort & Casino
11000 Broadway Boulevard SE
Albuquerque, NM 87105
505-724-3800
isleta.com

This resort appeared in *Breaking Bad* as a recovery center where Jesse Pinkman goes to struggle with his meth addiction. The Pinkman scenes were shot at the pool area, which has a distinctive, onion-like cabana.

The resort is also home to a golf course and bowling alley.

SELECTED FILMOGRAPHY

Blechynden, Frederik, camera. *Indian Day School*. USA: Thomas A. Edison, Inc, 1898. Video. https://www.loc.gov/item/00564534.

Griffith, D. W., dir. *A Pueblo Legend*. USA: Biograph Company, 1912. Film.

33

MOUNTAINAIR AND ENVIRONS

A funky little railroad town complete with centuries of history.

In 1903, Mountainair was officially incorporated and named for the breeze that flowed off the Manzano Mountains in the hopes that the town would become a valuable stopping point along the new Belen cutoff of the Atchison, Topeka & Santa Fe Railway. The railroad made farming and ranching much easier, so many villages reorganized themselves in an attempt to attract the railways, as Mountainair did. For a time, with the railroad to aid it, Mountainair claimed to be the "Pinto Bean Capitol of the World," but a drought just after World War II ended their reign.

Mountainair's growth presented opportunity and attracted hopeful entrepreneurs including Clem Shaffer, who migrated to New Mexico with his family from Indiana. The family tried their luck at farming and photography before their home burned down in 1922. Needing both a new home and a new source of income, the Shaffers decided to give the hotel business a try.

They purchased a lot near the train station and transformed it into a hotel with a Ford car dealership in the lobby. The hotel did well enough that the Shaffers were able to expand it just six years after it opened. Clem, usually called "Pop," developed a singular appreciation for making art and turned the hotel's dining room into an eclectic explosion of color. The dining room still operates.

Among the early films made in Mountainair, the short-form documentary *Unusual Occupations* captured a few minutes of Pop Shaffer at work making a wooden zoo. It was a propaganda film meant to capture the lives of Americans who were finding strange ways to make a living during the war years.

Some thirty years later, *Bobbie Jo and the Outlaw* swung by

HOW TO GET THERE

Mountainair is located off US Route 60, which can be reached via Interstate 25 or Interstate 40. From Interstate 40, take New Mexico State Road 337 south for 54 miles. From I-25, take New Mexico State Road 47 to US 60, then head east for twenty-one miles.

WHERE TO EAT

Alpine Alley Café
210 North Summit Avenue
Mountainair, NM 87036
505-847-2478
alpinealleycafe.com

Mountainair for a haircut scene. The film featured Lynda Carter as an aspiring country singer who links up with a man who wants to be the next Billy the Kid. Lynda Carter is best known for her superhero turn as Wonder Woman on television.

The Netflix global intelligence thriller *Messiah* also shot in Mountainair. The series follows a Christ figure who might or might not be a terrorist. After wrapping in New Mexico, the series went on to shoot in Jordan.

Nearby Estancia was once the center of a regional salt trade. Several Native American groups harvested and exchanged the salt with tribes as far away as Taos. When the Spanish colonized the area, they called the area "Salinas," or salt lake. Films including *2 Guns* and *Hell or High Water* visited the salt basin to shoot a few scenes, taking advantage of the white flats, open spaces, and clear blue skies.

The Salinas Pueblo Missions National Monument (105 South Ripley Street, Mountainair, NM, 87036; 505-847-2585, nps.gov/sapu) contains three well-preserved seventeenth-century missions. Although all three missions were abandoned in relatively short order, the ruins are extensive and provide an excellent snapshot of history.

SELECTED FILMOGRAPHY

Lester, Mark L., dir. *Bobbie Jo and the Outlaw*. USA: American International Pictures, 1976. Film.

34

BELEN

Once called "The Hub City," this small community south of Albuquerque has a Main Street appeal.

Spanish for "Bethlehem," Belen was founded on Spanish land grants in 1740 as "Nuestra Senora de Belen." Over time, the town grew around eight dispersed and quiet plazas. The railroad, though, changed the dynamic of the small town when it arrived in 1880. Little Belen was transformed into a bustling stopover almost overnight. The completion of the Belen cutoff in 1908 permanently tied the old Spanish village to the railroad. This new cutoff made the trip from Chicago to California much speedier.

Modern Belen has wide-open streets and several historic blocks attractive to moviemakers, who first arrived in 1971 with a comedy called *Bunny O'Hare*. The movie stars Bette Davis as a down-and-out older woman whose children have spent all of her life savings. She talks Ernest Borgnine into brushing up on the finer arts of robbery, and soon the two are pulling off heists together dressed as a hippie couple. Borgnine later returned to Belen with a character on the other side of law in *Convoy*. In that film Borgnine plays a sheriff hot on the tail of rogue, long-distance truckers.

More recently, *The Last Stand* brought Arnold Schwarzenegger and his deputies to Belen as they chase after a single driver, an escaped drug kingpin hauling butt across the American West in a modified Corvette. If the kingpin makes it past Belen, he'll reach safety and his cartel in Mexico. Schwarzenegger's deputies do what they can, but it falls to Schwarzenegger himself to stop the villain. The two throw down on a bridge across the border. After a decade spent as the governor of California, *The Last Stand* was

Ernest Borgnine and Bette Davis take a break on the set of *Bunny O'Hare* (1971). Courtesy of the Paul Andrew Hutton Collection and American International Pictures.

Ad for *Bunny O'Hare* (1971). Courtesy of the Paul Andrew Hutton Collection and American International Pictures.

meant to be Schwarzenegger's comeback vehicle into lead roles.

The historic Belen Hotel (200 Becker Avenue, Belen, NM, 87002) is visible for much of the shootout in *The Last Stand*. Built in 1907 for railroad workers, the Hotel had eighteen rooms, two stores, and a café. The hotel was recently renovated by artist Judy Chicago to serve as a private residence but is not open to the public.

The Belén Harvey House Museum (104 North 1st Street, Belen, NM, 87002; 505-861-0581, harveyhousemuseum.org), also a remnant of the railroad boom, has an exhibit on film history that features costumes and props from a handful of films that shot in the city. The rest of the museum is dedicated to the heyday of the Harvey House and the Fred Harvey empire.

HOW TO GET THERE

Belen is about forty minutes south of Albuquerque on Interstate 25.

WHERE TO STAY

Belen has several chain motels and hotels near the freeway.

WHERE TO EAT

Pete's Café
105 North 1st Street
Belen, NM 87002
505-864-4811
petescafenewmexico.com

SELECTED FILMOGRAPHY

Kim, Jee-woon, dir. *The Last Stand*. USA: Lionsgate, 2013. Film.

Oswald, Gerd, dir. *Bunny O'Hare*. USA: American International Pictures, 1971. Film.

An African village in *Sundown* (1941). Courtesy of the Paul Andrew Hutton Collection and United Artists.

35

ACOMA PUEBLO

One of the oldest, continuously inhabited villages in North America, Acoma is also a scenic and naturally occurring fortress. My Name Is Nobody *shot at the Pueblo in the early 1970s.*

Acoma defies gravity. Built atop a mesa that juts almost four hundred feet straight out of the desert floor, the Pueblo's fortress-like position draws comparisons with Masada in Israel. With no nearby water or arable land atop the mesa, it was, and continues to be, an impressive feat to live in such an isolated location, but the Acomans have made it work for almost a millennium. Even today, the people who live in "Sky City," as it's known, have no running water or grid electricity.

Because of its natural beauty and unique geography, Acoma appeared in films relatively early. In search of authenticity, producers of the film *Redskin* shot at Acoma Pueblo and in parts of the Navajo Nation. Ostensibly about an intertribal relationship and the challenges that Native Americans faced in the modern era, the film attempted to make a profound statement about the Native experience.

Henry Fonda at Acoma Pueblo in *My Name is Nobody* (1973).
Courtesy of Rafran Cinematografica.

PUEBLOS

New Mexico is home to nineteen inhabited Native American Pueblos, mostly located along the Rio Grande. The people of the Pueblos speak five different languages and have lived in the greater Rio Grande area for thousands of years.

Many New Mexican Pueblos welcome visitors but ask that certain etiquette be observed. Parts of the Pueblos are active sites of worship and should not be disturbed. Most Pueblos ask that visitors obtain a permit prior to taking photographs.

Almost all the Pueblos hold traditional dances and celebratory Feast Days, which are often open for anyone to attend. The Indian Pueblo Cultural Center in Albuquerque publishes an updated list of events at indianpueblo.org/19-pueblos. It's important to keep in mind that these events are often religious in nature, and guests should conduct themselves accordingly. Please never enter anyone's home without an invitation, and remember that Native American reservations are sovereign nations with their own governments and laws.

To accommodate the filming crew at isolated Acoma, the production built the first road to the top of the mesa. Prior to the road, most people had used one of several ancient trails carved into the soft stone. Amazingly, traditional residents had climbed up these rough trails while carrying water and other supplies for the town's entire history. The road built for *Redskin* was later upgraded for 1941's *Sundown*.

B-movie legend and director Roger Corman shot parts of his mixed-genre comedy *Gas-s-s-s: AKA Gas!—Or—It Became Necessary to Destroy the World in Order to Save It* around Acoma. The film follows survivors of a gas crisis that kills anyone over the age of twenty-five and was something of a reaction to a growing fear of hippies around the country. The renegade youth in the film respond to the emergency by taking a wild road trip across the country. The strange romp marked the last film that Corman would make with American International Pictures. (Often regarded as a genius of B-filmmaking, Corman mentored many successful directors including James Cameron, Francis Ford Coppola, Ron Howard, and many others.)

Terence Hill, who would later make a number of films in the Santa Fe area, visited Acoma briefly to work on *My Name Is Nobody*. Sergio Leone, famed for *The Man with no Name* trilogy,

EL MALPAIS NATIONAL MONUMENT

Less than an hour away from Acoma, El Malpais National Monument (1900 East Santa Fe Avenue, Grants, NM, 87020; 505-876-2783, nps.gov/elma) is checkered with dried lava flows from an ancient volcanic eruption. The lava created massive tubes and caves that visitors can hike inside, around, and through. Many of the caves require equipment and spelunking knowledge. Several, like Junction Cave, can be easily entered on foot. Above-ground options include the challenging Zuni-Acoma Trail. About 7.5 miles in each direction, the hike is best set up as a shuttle with a car parked at the end of the trail.

HOW TO GET THERE

Take Interstate 40 west to exit 102, then cross over the freeway and follow signs for Sky City Cultural Center.

Sky City Cultural Center &
Haak'u Museum
Haaku Road
Pueblo of Acoma, NM 87034
505-552-7861
acomaskycity.org

WHERE TO STAY

Sky City Casino Hotel
7 Sky City Drive
Pueblo of Acoma, NM 87034
505-552-6123
skycity.com

starring Clint Eastwood, came up with the concept for the film, but the movie was mostly made by Tonino Valerii and funded by a multinational European film endeavor. Henry Fonda and Terence Hill appear in a sequence with sweeping views of the solitary mesa and the valley below.

Any visit to the Pueblo should start at the new Sky City Cultural Center. The center includes a museum with changing exhibitions and is the starting point for guided tours to the mesa top. Tours are usually led by a local guide and include a short walk atop the mesa with historical highlights and handcrafted art for sale. At the conclusion of the tour, guests are offered an opportunity to walk down one of the traditional, steep trails or take the bus back along the road.

SELECTED FILMOGRAPHY

Corman, Roger, dir. *Gas-s-s-s: AKA Gas!—Or—It Became Necessary to Destroy the World in Order to Save It*. USA: American International Pictures, 1970. Film.

Hathaway, Henry, dir. *Sundown*. USA: Walter Wanger Productions, 1941. Film.

Scherzinger, Victor, dir. *Redskin*. USA: Paramount Pictures, 1929. Film.

Valerii, Tonino, dir. *My Name is Nobody*. Spain: Rafran Cinematografica, 1973. Film.

36

TO'HAJIILEE

These cliffs were made famous by Breaking Bad.

The deep-red and orange cliffs of To'hajiilee are unmistakably southwestern and immortalized by *Breaking Bad*. A writer for *Entertainment Weekly* called the remote area "perhaps the most important place in *Breaking Bad*'s mythology. It's where Jesse and Walt first cooked together. It's where Walt hid his money from the world. And it's where Todd, Jack, and the rest of the white-power Nazis get into a shootout with Hank and Gomez that leaves all of their fates up in the air."

A noncontiguous part of the Navajo Nation, To'hajiilee straddles several county lines and is directly west of Albuquerque on Interstate 40. The land was initially settled by a band of Navajo people after the Long Walk, a forced migration of the Navajo people from their traditional homelands near the Four Corners to an oppressive reservation at Bosque Redondo in the southern New Mexico Territory. The Canoncito Band of Navajos were able to avoid Bosque Redondo by covertly settling near a spring at To'hajilee.

In addition to *Breaking Bad* and *Better Call Saul*, the To'hajiilee scenery can be seen in several Tony Hillerman adaptations. Once a newspaper reporter and editor, Hillerman wrote mystery novels featuring Navajo characters living largely in the Navajo Nation. His books were bestsellers and brought Navajo culture and beliefs to an international audience. Robert Redford produced three movie adaptations of Hillerman's books.

CREW MEMORY

In a word, HOT. It was July. The shoot was supposed to take nine days. . . . I think it ended up taking eighteen. I can't remember

HOW TO GET THERE

To'hajiilee Chapter Office
117 Tribal Rd N7071
To'hajiilee, NM 87026
505-908-2730

Off Interstate 40, take exit 131 and proceed north for 6.3 miles.

This location is on private land that belongs to the tribe. It can only be reached on dirt roads and is not accessible at all times. Visitors are asked to check in with the To'hajiilee Chapter Office prior to their visit. As on all tribal lands, visitors are asked to be respectful during their stay. Do not climb any rock formations, block any roads, or gather any souvenirs.

One of the final episodes of *Breaking Bad* (2008–2013) is named "To'hajiilee." Courtesy of Sony Pictures Entertainment.

for sure; parts of my brain short-circuited after it reached 106 degrees. There were no trees to speak of, no water, just rocks and sun and DUST. Oh Lord, the dust! Little cyclones of dust would pop up out of nowhere like ghosts (what are they called? dust devils?) and wreak havoc on equipment, tents, and anything that was dumb enough to need to breathe oxygen. I would blow my nose at the end of the day, and it would just be brown. I would drink water constantly and never have to pee. As the days dragged on, everyone on the crew started to look the same—sun hats, sun shirts, and bandanas up to their eyes. We looked like a bunch of mummies ready to rob a bank.

We had a snake wrangler on set sitting there in her camping chair with her five-gallon bucket and one of those extender grabby things, and someone asked if she'd caught any snakes yet. She said, "Nah. It's too hot for snakes." That became a T-shirt. —*Anonymous*

SELECTED FILMOGRAPHY:

Eyre, Chris, dir. *A Thief of Time*. USA: Carlton International Media, Corporation for Public Broadcasting, Granada Entertainment, 2004. Film

Gilligan, Vince, creator. *Breaking Bad*. USA: American Movie Classics, 2008–2013. Television series.

Spaceport America is the United States' first commercial spaceport.
© istokphoto.com | Judd Irish Bradley.

37

TRUTH OR CONSEQUENCES AND THE NEW MEXICO SPACEPORT

The future site of commercial space travel is not far from a hot springs getaway.

Despite New Mexico's long history with film and television making, only one town is actually named after a show. The town of Hot Springs changed its name in 1950 to Truth or Consequences to honor the tenth anniversary of the radio show of the same name and the launch of a television-show adaptation. The show's host, Ralph Edwards, flew to New Mexico to visit the small town after the name officially changed and then returned almost every year until his death in 2005. The Geronimo Springs Museum (211 Main Street, Truth or Consequences, NM, 87901; 575-894-6600, geronimospringsmuseum.com) has an exhibit on the guests who appeared during the fiestas that accompanied Edwards's annual visit.

Hot Springs was actually a more apt name for the town thanks to a rift that formed below the Rio Grande that pushes hot water toward the surface. These springs became popular after a construction boom at nearby Elephant Butte brought hordes of hopeful gamblers and healers to the area in the early twentieth century. Tented bath houses popped up along the river, giving good cause to name the upstart town Hot Springs. Today, ten hot springs and bath houses are available in the small city. Some have attached hotels, and others are located right on the Rio Grande.

A crime drama starring Kiefer Sutherland took the name of the town as its title in 1997. While *Truth or Consequences, N.M.*, is supposed to unfold in the New Mexico town, the film was mostly shot in Utah and Nevada. The Disney+ teen romance *Stargirl* used the streets of Truth or Consequences briefly for a walking shot.

HOW TO GET THERE

Truth or Consequences is located off Interstate 25, about 150 miles south of Albuquerque.

Spaceport America
County Road A021
Truth or Consequences, NM 87901
575-267-8500
spaceportamerica.com

Spaceport America is only open to visitors on tours or with special authorization.

WHERE TO STAY

Sierra Grande
501 McAdoo Street
Truth or Consequences, NM 87901
tedturnerreserves.com/sierra-grande

The hotel is owned by media magnate Ted Turner.

WHERE TO DRINK

Truth or Consequences Brewing Company
410 North Broadway
Truth or Consequences, NM 87901
575-297-0289
torc.beer

In addition to the hot springs, Truth or Consequences is also home to the Spaceport America Visitor Center (301 South Foch Street, Truth or Consequences, NM, 87901; 575-267-8888, spaceportamerica.com). Tours to the spaceport itself begin at this location or in Las Cruces. Please check availability on their website (spaceportamerica.com/visit).

The spaceport is a joint venture between Virgin Galactic and the State of New Mexico and is scheduled to become the first facility in the world to offer commercial, passenger space flight. A decade old at press time, it has yet to launch a civilian into space. Instead, it has become an active research center for aerospace development and emerging technologies for companies like Exos Aerospace, Boeing, White Sands Missile Range, and the Commercial Spaceflight Federation.

The futuristic design of the spaceport made it a great choice for a sequence in the sci-fi film *The Space Between Us*. The film follows a teen born and raised in space who steals away to earth to go on a road trip with a girl he met online. Much of the film shot at I-25 Studio, but a few of the opening minutes were shot on location at the spaceport. At the time, it was the first production to visit the building.

For more earthly activities, nearby Elephant Butte Lake State Park (101 State Road 195 Elephant Butte, NM, 87935; 575-744-5923, www.emnrd.state.nm.us/spd/elephantbuttelakestatepark.html) is a popular weekend escape for New Mexicans. The lake is accessible for boating, hiking, and fishing when the weather permits.

SELECTED FILMOGRAPHY

Chelsoem, Peter, dir. *The Space Between Us*. USA: STX Entertainment, 2017. Film.

Edwards, Ralph, creator. *The New Truth and Consequences*. USA: CBS, National Broadcasting Company, Ralph Edwards Productions, 1950–1988.

Radio telescopes in the Very Large Array near Soccorro.
© istokphoto.com | Greg Meland.

38

VERY LARGE ARRAY (VLA)

The collection of radio telescopes used for astronomy allowed for Jodie Foster to communicate with extraterrestrials in the film Contact, *which was based on the novel by Carl Sagan.*

The opening frames—and later the advertising materials—of the 1997 film *Contact* feature a focused Jodie Foster listening intently to headphones. Behind her, massive radio telescope dishes point toward the sky. The dishes in this film are just a small segment of New Mexico's Very Large Array (VLA).

The VLA bills itself as "one of the world's premier astronomical radio observatories," featuring twenty-seven large dishes that give scientists a better look at the stars. The dishes are each eighty-two feet in diameter, and their imaging can be collectively assembled. The VLA is jointly operated by the National Science Foundation and Associated Universities, Inc.

Naturally, the VLA is a great fit for science-fiction films. The dishes can move simultaneously and create an eerie effect. The VLA

Movie tie-in edition of Carl Sagan's *Contact*. Courtesy of the Paul Andrew Hutton Collection.

is also picturesque because it stands almost alone on the Plains of San Agustin. A handful of films have used short clips of the VLA including *Transformers*, *Transcendence*, *Terminator Salvation*, and *2010* (the rarely discussed sequel to Stanley Kubrick's *2001: A Space Odyssey*).

Famed astronomer and television personality Carl Sagan first visited the VLA in 1979 while working on his television show *Cosmos*. (A second incarnation of the show would later shoot in New Mexico. This updated rendition used the Santa Fe Studios as its base and shot all over the state. Astrophysicist Neil DeGrasse Tyson assumed Carl Sagan's role in the series.) The impressive dishes and operation stuck in Sagan's memory, and the facility played a part in his novel *Contact*. The hero of the book, Eleanor Arroway, works for the Search for Extraterrestrial Intelligence (SETI) Institute and uses the VLA to scan the universe for alien communications. The VLA is mentioned by name in the text.

Before the novel was published, Sagan shared a draft with friend and producer Lynda Obst. The story underwent multiple revisions and incarnations before Obst finally got the green light for a movie rendition in 1993. The Studio hired George Miller—of *Mad Max* and *Babe* fame—to direct, then they parted ways with him because their ideas for the film never gelled. Hot off the Academy Award–winning *Forrest Gump*, director Robert Zemeckis took over. Zemeckis and his team entered the project with tempered expectations. As Zemeckis put it, "No matter how successful this movie ends up being, it's always going to fall short of *Gump*. I've had to resign myself to that. To quote Carl Sagan, the mathematical probability that I would ever make a movie like *Gump* again is pretty nil."

The VLA would have a role in the film, but Zemeckis and his team weren't initially certain that they would film on site in New Mexico. After scouting, Zemeckis was taken with the array and brought the production to the isolated research center. The complex operations of the VLA immediately presented problems for the film. The crew wanted to move the dishes into a more picturesque formation, but that would have interrupted research. Even the basic equipment that a crew normally used threatened to interrupt the dishes. The VLA and the production eventually reached a compromise, though.

HOW TO GET THERE

State Road 60 (the VLA has no physical address)
Magdalena, NM 87825
GPS Coordinates:
34 04'43.497N, 107 37'05.819W
public.nrao.edu/visit/very-large-array

Admission fees apply.

WHERE TO STAY

Nearby Socorro has several chain motels and hotels.

WHERE TO EAT

Socorro Springs Restaurant
1012 North California Street
Socorro, NM 87801
575-838-0650
socorrosprings.com

The crew shot for a week at the VLA, but instead of using the actual control room, filmmakers built two simulated rooms to use as sets. One they constructed on stage in Los Angeles, and the other they built close to the VLA itself, because designers wanted to mimic the actual control room closely. The film also received a limited window to reposition the dishes.

Contact also shot in Los Angeles, Puerto Rico, Florida, and Arizona. Released in 1997, the film earned 170 million dollars at the worldwide box office. As Zemeckis suspected, the success of *Contact* fell far short of *Forrest Gump*, but it was a decent return on a film that grappled with difficult concepts and didn't indulge in the typical tropes of alien movies.

The VLA is open to visitors on the first and third Saturday of each month for tours. Included in the tour is a video introduction to the VLA with narration by Jodie Foster. The Visitor Center is open every day.

Nearby, the Bosque Del Apache National Wildlife Refuge Center (1001 New Mexico State Road 1, San Antonio, NM, 87832; 575-835-1828) is a seasonal home for a variety of migratory birds. Birdwatchers can catch a glimpse of flycatchers, quail, or sandhill cranes as they pass through. Each season brings different wildlife, so check ahead on weather and conditions.

SELECTED FILMOGRAPHY

Bay, Michael, dir. *Transformers: The Movie*. USA: Paramount Pictures, 2007. Film.

Hyams, Peter, dir. *2010*. USA: Metro-Goldwyn-Mayer, 1984. Film.

McG, dir. *Terminator Salvation*. USA: Warner Bros., 2009. Film.

Pfister, Wally, dir. *Transcendence*. USA: Alcon Entertainment, Warner Bros., 2014. Film.

Sagan, Carl, Ann Druyan, and Steven Soter, creators. *Cosmos: A Personal Voyage*. USA: Public Broadcasting Service, 1980. Television series.

Zemeckis, Robert, dir. *Contact*. USA: Warner Bros., 1997. Film.

39

GALLUP

On the edge of the Navajo Reservation,
Gallup was once a popular destination for filmmakers.
John Wayne and Peter Fonda visited to shoot
the nearby rock formations.

With *Sunset Boulevard*, writer and director Billy Wilder sharply reprimanded the dark but dreamy culture of contemporary Hollywood. The film, now considered a classic, struck nerves in show business. Undeterred, Wilder followed his dismantling of the film business with a sharp critique of journalism and its ethics. In *Ace in the Hole* Kirk Douglas plays a reporter marooned in Albuquerque. Douglas's character, Chuck Tatum, dreams of finding the big story that will get him back to the big time.

Instead, Tatum finds only boring rattlesnake hunts and other small-town stories not worth his talents. Then, he happens upon an accident at the Minosa Trading Post in fictional Escadero, New Mexico. Tatum finds that Leo Minosa, owner of the trading post, is trapped by a cave-in deep underneath an ancient cliff dwelling. Tatum thinks it's the perfect story and takes control of the situation. Ultimately, Tatum will have to decide if human life is worth more than a national headline.

Wilder and his writing partner found inspiration for the film in two real-life stories. In San Marino, California, in 1949, a child fell into an open well, sparking a media circus and drawing thousands of people to watch as emergency personnel attempted a rescue. In the 1920s in Kentucky, a cave explorer found himself trapped and created a buzz for national headlines. Both tragedies were a form of the human-interest story—which was the original title of Wilder's film.

Kirk Douglas and Jan Sterling in *Ace in the Hole* (1951). Courtesy of the Paul Andrew Hutton Collection and Paramount Pictures.

DRIVE WHERE SUPERMAN FLEW

Decades before comic book films dominated the world box office, New Mexico hosted one of the signature early superhero flicks. In 1978, the first of the Christopher Reeve *Superman* films shot near Gallup. After archvillain Lex Luthor detonates an atomic bomb in the San Andreas Fault, earthquakes tear apart the West Coast. Margot Kidder as Lois Lane gets trapped in a rift and ultimately killed. To shoot the scene in which her car is buried under a rockslide, the crew traveled to a spot just north of Gallup, now called Superman Canyon Road. Take Hasler Valley Road out of Gallup to see it.

Filming started in Albuquerque and then moved to Gallup. Using a real alcove, the crew built a replica Native American cliff dwelling that cost the studio some thirty thousand dollars (the interior of the cave was built and shot on stage in Los Angeles). The structure stood at 235 feet high, 1,200 feet across, and 1,600 feet deep—including the cliff, roadside stands, a parking lot for five hundred cars, and kiddie rides, booths, and concession stands. All in all, "Paramount's public relations team claimed [this] was the largest noncombat set ever constructed." Unfortunately, there's nothing left of the set, and the alcove is on private property off New Mexico 118, just under three miles from the Arizona border.

Another natural formation in the Gallup area, Red Rock Park is open to the public and easy to visit. Red Rock shows up in a number of Westerns including *Fort Defiance*, *Desert Song*, and *El Paso*. The park has

The Gallup set of *Ace in the Hole* (1951). Courtesy of the Paul Andrew Hutton Collection and Paramount Pictures.

HISTORICAL GRAFFITI

El Morro National Monument (New Mexico State Road 53, Ramah, NM, 87321; 505-783-4226 x801, nps.gov/elmo) is an ancient watering hole complete with more than a millennium of graffiti carved into the stone. Often called "Inscription Rock," the cliffside at El Morro has elaborate written carvings made by Native peoples, Spanish conquistadors, and traveling pioneers. A short trail winds around the mesa and up to the top.

One of the inscriptions at El Morro became the inspiration for the Eugene Manlove Rhodes novel *Pasó por Aquí*. The novel was later adapted into a film starring real-life married couple Joel McCrea and Frances Dee called *Four Faces West*. They filmed on site at El Morro.

To get there, take New Mexico State Road 53 south from Gallup for forty-two miles.

a museum, a campground, and trails. Red Rock Park also hosts marquee events like the Gallup Inter-Tribal Indian Ceremonial and local and national rodeo competitions.

Red Rock Park was only part of the draw for early Westerns. Gallup also had a location convenient to the railroad, Route 66, and other scenic shooting locations like Monument Valley. Built in 1881 along the tracks of the Atlanta and Pacific line, Gallup took the name of a railroad paymaster who worked in the area. At first just a service stop, the small town quickly became a major exporter of coal and wood products.

The railroads also moved tourists, many of whom spurred interest in Native Americana. As a result, Santa Fe and Albuquerque blossomed into centers of the Native-art trade and visitation, with Gallup following behind them. That trend continued when Route 66, and then Interstate 40, were charted past Gallup.

Gallup also borders on the Navajo Nation and is close to Zuni Pueblo, making it as much a cultural intersection as it is a physical one. The evolving tourist trade made Gallup an important market for Native American art. A number of historical trading posts are still in business there. A few places to try for Native art include the Ellis Tanner Trading Company (1980 New Mexico State Road 602, Gallup, NM, 87301; 505-863-4434, etanner.com) and the Perry Null Trading Company (1710 South 2nd Street, Gallup, NM, 87301; 505-863-5249, perrynulltrading.com).

One of the first major commercial films to stop in Gallup capitalized on Native American themes and locations. In 1929 *Redskin* used Acoma and Gallup. Many other films and a procession of A-list stars soon followed.

R. E. "Griff" Griffith, the famous director's brother, liked Gallup enough that he decided to make a permanent investment in the town. Griffith built the El Rancho Hotel as a rustic, roadside attraction. He even brought in former Harvey House employees to ensure that customer service was state of the art. A neon sign above the entrance to the hotel promised that El Rancho had the "Charm of Yesterday" and the "Convenience of Tomorrow."

To ensure their better tomorrow, the Griffiths convinced Los Angeles–based productions to use the hotel as a base for making Westerns. The explosion of Western filmmaking fit their plans perfectly. The lobby of the hotel is packed with photos of the many movie stars who

HOW TO GET THERE

Close to the border with Arizona, Gallup can be reached on Interstate 40 or by its regional airport.

WHERE TO STAY

El Rancho Hotel
1000 East US Route 66
Gallup, NM 87301
505-863-9311
elranchohotelgallup.com

WHERE TO EAT

Jerry's Cafe
406 West Coal Avenue
Gallup, NM 87301
505-722-6775

visited. John Wayne, Jane Fonda, Gregory Peck, Rita Hayworth, Humphrey Bogart, and many other superstars stayed at the hotel during filming.

Less than ten years after Griffith developed the El Rancho, he built another hotel in Las Vegas, Nevada, called the Last Frontier. One of the early resort hotels in Las Vegas, the hotel would eventually be owned by Howard Hughes and would play a small part in the careers of Liberace and hotel magnate Steve Wynn. For its part, the El Rancho is still a functional hotel and motel with a restaurant and bar. It's a must-see for cinephiles.

SELECTED FILMOGRAPHY

Florey, Robert, dir. *Desert Song*. USA: Warner Bros., 1943. Film.

Foster, Lewis, dir. *El Paso*. USA: Paramount Pictures, 1949. Film.

Green, Alfred E., dir. *Four Faces West*. USA: United Artists, 1948. Film.

Rawlins, John, dir. *Fort Defiance*. USA: United Artists, 1951. Film.

Wilder, Billy, dir. *Ace in the Hole*. USA: Paramount Pictures, 1951. Film.

PART VI

SOUTHERN NEW MEXICO

Johnny Mack Brown in *Billy the Kid* (1930).
Courtesy of the Paul Andrew Hutton Collection
and Metro-Goldwyn Mayer.

40

LINCOLN AND RUIDOSO

Billy the Kid made the area famous, but almost all the films about the outlaw shot elsewhere.

The tiny town of Lincoln might have come and gone in relative obscurity were it not for the capital ambitions of two Europeans who hoped to make a significant profit in the town. These dueling mercantilists both aimed to make a profit off the United States Army. Their competition became aggressive and eventually violent in the late 1800s.

Both sides of the feud found refuge in the law, and both attracted men with established resumes of extreme brutality. The men organized into posses, the most famous of which was called the Regulators and featured a buck-toothed, gangly young man known by several names including Henry McCarty, Henry Antrim, and William H. Bonney. As the fighting escalated, the feud took on a name, and so did its most famous fighter, Billy the Kid, who survived the Lincoln County War only to be shot in the middle of the night by lawman Pat Garrett.

Despite his relative fame, details on Bonney's life are scant. He was probably born in 1859 in New York City. At some point he migrated west with his mother and eventually arrived at Silver City, where his mother ran a boarding house. As a teenager Bonney absconded to Arizona, where he killed his first man. On the lam, he returned to New Mexico and to the Lincoln County area, where he found work as a ranch hand. Stories of his part in the Lincoln County War made him an object of intrigue and curiosity throughout the New Mexico Territory. But his death is what made him a celebrity.

In the years after Sheriff Pat Garrett gunned him down in 1881, Bonney transformed from a famed outlaw into a fictional, perhaps mythical, character who appeared in almost every medium. Bonney became the subject of many newspaper articles and then of dime novels. He was a natural lead subject for film in the early days of the industry.

Some seventy films and television shows feature versions of the Billy the Kid legend, making him one of the most popular celluloid characters in American history. Paul Newman played Billy, as did Emilio Estevez and Roy Rogers. John Wayne never played Billy, but he did play a cattle baron who happened to know Billy. At one point, Bonney even shared screen time with Dracula. And in a cartoon series, Bonney was anthropomorphized as a baby goat—that is, a kid.

Most of these Billy the Kid films chose to shoot outside of historic Lincoln because it is too isolated and small for most production teams. 1989's *Young Guns* shot in Cerrillos (see location 7) while 1930's *Billy the Kid* shot in Gallup. As of press time, the most recent Billy the Kid film, *The Kid*, filmed around Santa Fe. Another was in development and planned to shoot in Calgary, Alberta.

Now a New Mexico Historic Site (nmhistoricsites.org/lincoln), Lincoln looks much as it did in the late 1800s when Bonney and his compatriots tore through it. The famed courthouse where the Kid engineered his best-known escape is still standing, as is the store where Bonney was once trapped and almost killed.

Lincoln features seventeen historic structures, including two museums and a well-preserved mercantile store that is complete with period goods in their original displays. Most of the buildings are visible on a short walking tour. Not all of them are open year-round, and visitors should check ahead before they go.

From Lincoln, the Billy the Kid Scenic Byway (newmexico.org/places-to-visit/scenic-byways/billy-the-kid) makes a loop around the Lincoln National Forest past some significant and odd landmarks. One of these landmarks is for another icon from the area, Smokey Bear, whose legend was born just to the east of Lincoln in Capitan. After a forest fire, a bear cub emerged from the embers alive and became the literal poster child for fire prevention. Smokey Bear Historical Park (118 West Smokey Bear Blvd, Capitan, NM, 88316; 575-354-2748, www.emnrd.state.nm.us/SFD/SmokeyBear/SmokeyBearPark.html) was erected in his honor in 1976. ("The" was added to Smokey's name for better rhyming in the popular children's song written about him.) The byway also passes near Fort Stanton (104 Kit Carson Road, Fort Stanton, NM, 88323; 575-354-0341, fortstanton.org), where the United States Army once kept watch over local Apaches. It is now a New Mexico State Monument.

Follow the byway on to Ruidoso (pronounced "re-a-dough-so"), which is home to Ski Apache (1286 Ski Run Road, Alto, NM, 88312; 575-464-3600, skiapache.com) and the Hubbard Museum of the American West (26301 US Route 70, Ruidoso Downs, NM, 88346; 575-378-4142, hubbardmuseum.org). Allow two hours for the eighty-four-mile drive. A few productions have used Ruidoso for outdoors shots, primarily in Westerns. *Into the West*, with writing and producing by Emmy Award–winning New Mexico resident Kirk Ellis, shot in the foothills near Ruidoso. The six-part miniseries garnered seventeen Emmy Award nominations and also featured footage shot at Eaves and Bonanza Creek Ranch.

The Christian end times thriller *The Prodigal Planet* shot at the Fox Caves in Ruidoso. The film follows a group of believers awaiting the return of Christ after the Antichrist has all but destroyed the earth. The Fox Cave itself as a histor-

HOW TO GET THERE

Located off US Route 380.

WHERE TO STAY

Accommodations are available in nearby Ruidoso or Capitan.

WHERE TO EAT

The Dolan House
826 Calle La Placita
Lincoln, NM 88338
575-653-4670
thedolanhouse.com

ical and geological oddity, a deep opening carved into soft limestone by years of hydrologic erosion. It's now home to something of a curiosities shop that deals all kinds of miscellany (26897 US Route 70, Ruidoso Downs, NM, 88346; 575-378-9954).

SELECTED FILMOGRAPHY

Thompson, Donald W., dir, *The Prodigal Planet*. USA: Mark IV Pictures, Inc., 1983. Film.

Ellis, Kirk, producer. *Into the West*. USA: TNT/Dreamworks Television, 2005. TV series.

41

ROSWELL

The site of a supposed alien landing, the town itself is a pop-culture phenomenon.

On the map, Roswell sits between the mountains and the plains. On film and in pop culture, it exists between science fiction and Westerns.

The small city sprang up after the Civil War on the strength of local ranches. John Chisum, who eventually became involved in the Lincoln County War, owned property near the nascent town. Later, the discovery of water and the arrival of the railroad at the end of the nineteenth century brought in an era of modernization. Military activity and supposed alien activity in the twentieth century spurred additional growth.

The alien-landing hubbub began in 1947 when a couple of Roswell-area ranchers were driving across their acreage. They discovered a mysterious pile of wreckage that they couldn't explain. They brought it to local law enforcement, looking for an answer. The sheriff, in turn, contacted the military, hoping for more information. Perhaps because they didn't want to expose their secretive Project Mogul, the military allowed reports of alien Unidentified Flying Objects to go to print. The patently false reports, nonetheless, gained traction.

Over the course of decades, and despite contradictory evidence, rumors of an alien landing persisted. The story erupted in pop culture to the degree that the CW network ran a successful series on aliens in a small town called *Roswell*. Years later, they rebooted the show. Neither rendition filmed in Southern New Mexico, although the second series shot in Albuquerque and Santa Fe.

Roswell is home to several alien-themed attractions like the International UFO Museum & Research Center (114 North Main

The NMMI campus in *The Men Who Stare at Goats* (2009). Courtesy of Overture Films.

Street Roswell, NM, 88203; 575-625-9495, roswellufomuseum.com). Opened in 1992, the museum offers comprehensive resources on a number of UFO-related incidents from crop circles to Area 51 (which is located in Nevada, not New Mexico).

For a slightly more grounded, but still aerial, exploration of vehicular travel and weapons development in the area, try the Walker Aviation Museum (1 Jerry Smith Circle, Roswell, NM, 88201, 575-347-2464, wafbmuseum.org). The Roswell Army Air Field and Walker Air Force Base both played an integral part in twentieth-century weapons development. The Air Field also played a part in the birth of the UFO controversy.

Before science fiction had an impact on Roswell, Westerns made use of the plains town. Gene Autry visited in the late 1940s with the aptly titled *Sons of New Mexico*, which made use of the venerable New Mexico Military Institute (NMMI).

Built at the close of the nineteenth century, NMMI confers high school and associate's degrees through the Reserve Officer Training Corps. It bills itself as "the nation's only state-supported co-educational military boarding school" and the "West Point of the West." It's also a grand Gothic Revival campus that can fill in for eastern universities in film.

The science-fiction comedy *The Men Who Stare at Goats* used the campus as the headquarters for their New Earth Army. Based loosely on a real story reported in a book of the same name, the film and book follow a Vietnam veteran who adapts and espouses parapsychology techniques to make warfare more peaceful. The trainees attempt mind control, running through walls, cloud bursting, and telekinetic goat murdering.

The film unfolds through the eyes of journalist Bob Wilton, who is played by Ewan McGregor. Wilton comes across Lyn Casady (George Clooney) while on assignment in Iraq, and Casady introduces Wilton to the secretive program and their dubious abilities. Jeff Bridges plays Bill Django—the mastermind of the project and the lead instructor of the school. NMMI is visible in a number of scenes in which he goes through his outlandish techniques. The General Douglas L. McBride Museum (101 West College Boule-

HOW TO GET THERE

Roswell can be reached by airport or on US Route 285.

WHERE TO STAY

Roswell has several chain motels and hotels.

WHERE TO EAT

Los Cerritos Mexican Kitchen
2103 North Main Street
Roswell, NM 88201
575-622-4919
loscerritosmk.com

vard, Roswell, NM, 88201; 800-421-5376 nmmi.edu/visiting-nmmi/campus-attractions/museum) recounts the history of the institute and is located on campus.

CREW MEMORY

Writer/director Sam Shepard shot his ghost Western *Silent Tongue*, starring River Phoenix and Dermot Mulroney, on ranches outside of Roswell in the early nineties. I visited the set to write about it for the *Los Angeles Times*, since I was a journalist then. The story was set on the harsh Llano Estacado in 1893. Shepard said, "This was probably the most terrifying piece of real estate west of the Mississippi. It was absolutely scary." During filming, transpo vans took actors and crew from one cactus-filled location to another, while Shepard just mounted a horse and rode on to the next location. —*Wolf Schneider, Unit Publicist*

SELECTED FILMOGRAPHY

English, John, dir. *Sons of New Mexico*. USA: Columbia Pictures, 1949. Film.

Heslov, Grant, dir. *The Men Who Stare at Goats*. USA: BBC Films, 2009. Film.

42

LAS CRUCES

Clint Eastwood made parts of two films in Las Cruces. In 1968, segments of Hang 'Em High *shot around Las Cruces. Fifty years later, Eastwood returned with* The Mule.

Early in *Hang 'Em High*, Clint Eastwood as Jed Cooper crosses the Rio Grande and runs into an angry posse. This group wrongfully convicts Cooper on the spot and hangs him from a cottonwood tree. Cooper is saved by a passerby and survives to become a local marshal and administer his own brand of justice. The film was the first that Eastwood made after the smashing success of the *Man with No Name* trilogy, in which Eastwood starred as the laconic, sneering gunslinger.

The success of the Sergio Leone–directed Spaghetti Westerns made Eastwood famous but not bankable in the United States. The studios were unsure that they could place Eastwood in a leading role in an American film. After all, he spent most of the Leone films in a stern silence. Eastwood took plenty of meetings in the year after his final Italian Western was made, but nothing definite materialized. He grew frustrated.

Eastwood took matters into his own hands with a script written by two of the voices behind the *Hawaii Five-O* television series. The *Hang 'Em High* script had just enough of the wordless fervor of the Leone films to keep their momentum going. It also offered a singular vision of Western justice. To maximize his potential earnings, Eastwood made the film under his own production company, Malpaso. The plan paid off and launched Eastwood's American film career.

Clint Eastwood gets dragged to his hanging in *Hang 'Em High* (1968).
Courtesy of the Paul Andrew Hutton Collection and United Artists.

Although Eastwood gave notes on the *Hang 'Em High* script and produced the film via Malpaso, it wasn't his from stem to stern. In the years after, though, Eastwood became one of the most celebrated directors and auteurs in Hollywood. Into his ninth decade, Eastwood maintained a reputation for quick decisions and fast shooting on set. *The Mule*, for which Eastwood returned to Las Cruces to shoot fifty years later, was entirely Eastwood's project. He starred in and directed the film about a retiree who takes a job running drugs for the cartel.

The Mule shot primarily in Georgia but used the Las Cruces area extensively. The Organ Mountains are clearly visible in a few road scenes. Bridging the gap between Georgia and Southern New Mexico, Eastwood's character hauls pecans to hide his stash of drugs. Turns out that Georgia is the biggest producer of pecans in the United States, and Southern New Mexico is the second largest.

The international narcotics market was also at the center of director Steven Soderbergh's *Traffic*. The Academy Award–winning meditation on the toll of the drug trade in the Americas featured the Las Cruces International Airport for a scene in which dangerous cargo is moved across the desert. Shot before the modern incentives were put in place, Soderbergh and crew chose Las Cruces for the desert look and not for the financial savings. (The Airport also made a brief appearance in the comedy *Twins*.)

Although prized by filmmakers for its desert skies and open landscape, New Mexico is rich in agriculture. In addition to pecans, Southern New Mexico is also known for growing green chiles—which show up on pretty much everything you eat there. Both crops and the greater agricultural industry are on display at the New Mexico Farm and Ranch Heritage Museum in Las Cruces (4100 Dripping Springs Road, Las Cruces, NM, 88011; 575-522-4100, nmfarmandranchmuseum.org). The museum also has changing exhibitions on local history.

The Organ Mountains—named for their resemblance to the pipes of a musical organ—feature a few hallmark hiking trails like the ones at Dripping Springs Natural Area (15000 Dripping Springs Road, Las Cruces, NM, 88005; 575-522-1219, blm.gov/visit

WHERE TO STAY

Hotel Encanto de las Cruces
705 South Telshor Boulevard
Las Cruces, NM 88011
575-522-4300
hotelencanto.com

WHERE TO EAT

La Posta de Mesilla
2410 Calle De San Albino
Mesilla, NM 88046
575-524-3524
lapostademesilla.com

Clint Eastwood was spotted here while working on *The Mule*.

/dripping-springs-natural-area), which wind past natural springs and the remnants of a century-old resort. The primary trail is about three miles long.

Just four miles south of Las Cruces, La Mesilla has a charming plaza and a collection of historic buildings, many of which date back to the mid-nineteenth century. The town was at the crossroads of several major trade lines including the El Camino Real, the San Antonio Mail, and Wells Fargo Express. The continuous trade attracted a steady stream of visitors to the town and not only kept the store fronts and traders afloat but also the saloons and theaters. Until the railroad arrived in Las Cruces in 1881, redirecting the trade traffic, Mesilla was the hot-spot gathering place.

Much of the historic plaza remains intact, and several of the businesses have been in operation for almost a century. The El Patio Bar (2171 Calle De Parian, Mesilla, NM, 88046; 575-526-9943), for instance, has served drinks in the same spot since the mid-1930s. La Posta de Mesilla opened just a few years later.

La Mesilla also appears briefly on film. It subbed in for Mexico in *Brokeback Mountain*.

SELECTED FILMOGRAPHY

Eastwood, Clint, dir. *The Mule*. USA: Warner Bros., 2018. Film.

Lee, Ang, dir. *Brokeback Mountain*. USA: Universal Pictures, 2005. Film.

Post, Ted, dir. *Hang 'Em High*. USA: United Artists, 1968. Film.

43

ARTESIA

David Bowie crash landed in this boomtown on the plains in The Man Who Fell to Earth.

Musician David Bowie had a long-standing fascination with space, evident in hits he wrote like "Space Oddity," "Starman," and "Life on Mars." He also performed concerts in character as Ziggy Stardust, an abstract alien messenger, after the release of his album *The Rise and Fall of Ziggy Stardust and the Spiders from Mars* in 1972. But it took more than a passing interest in science fiction for him to agree to his first starring film role in *The Man Who Fell to Earth*.

The trippy film, based on the book of the same name by Walter Tevis, follows the exploits of an alien who lands on earth. The alien takes the name Thomas Jerome Newton and hopes to use his technological skills to make money. With his amassed resources, Newton plans to find a way to ship water back to his home planet (it's a little ironic that he would search for water in New Mexico, but the production initially planned to shoot in Tennessee). In the process, Newton falls in love with a human woman and becomes entangled with earthly politics.

As much as it is science fiction, the film is also a study of the cost of invention. Newton, of course, is named after the physicist, but he has more in common with a famed aviator. "It's a bit like a Howard Hughes story," Bowie said in an interview. In a way, Newton also prefigured the tech innovators who would become larger than life in the decades after the film was released.

Bowie was something of a risk in the lead. Not only was he inexperienced as an actor, but he struggled with cocaine abuse. Some reports claimed that he told director Nic Roeg prior to shooting that he would stay sober only long enough to make the film. The addiction, perhaps, made Bowie paranoid. A fly in his cereal milk

David Bowie and Candy Clark sing at church in *The Man Who Fell to Earth* (1976). Courtesy of Cinema 5 Distributing.

on set one morning sent him into a panic over a fear of potential poisoning. The production came to a halt as a local hospital examined Bowie. His mental state added to his on-screen performance as an uncomfortable alien, though. "This guy doesn't need a lot of talk. He is Mr. Newton," said Roeg in a later interview.

On set, Bowie got along well with the crew, most of whom were British even though they shot in New Mexico. Despite the additional costs, Roeg and the producers opted to pay to bring their usual crew in from England. (New Mexico was a "right-to-work state" at the time, meaning that non-union crews could legally film in the state. New Mexico is now a "non-right-to-work" state, but not all film shoots are made under union agreements.) They all traveled together aboard a chartered Aer Lingus flight from London. Then they drove together all over New Mexico, making stops in Roswell, Albuquerque, Lake Fenton, and Artesia.

At first Artesia was solely a whistle-stop town along the train line. The discovery of deep aquifer supplies of water, though, transformed it. With a little bit of work, agriculture became a reality. Drilling rigs sprang up all over the area in the early 1900s to bring up the water for irrigation. When, by accident, one of the drills hit a pocket of oil, an oil boom was spurred, which doubled the size of small Artesia in the 1920s. Soon thereafter a refinery opened, making the oil presence somewhat permanent.

One remnant of the oil-business boom was the historic Hotel Artesia, built in 1929. The old building, scheduled for demolition when Roeg and his crew arrived, fit their needs per-

HOW TO GET THERE

Artesia sits on the southeastern corner of New Mexico at the crossing of US Routes 82 and 85.

WHERE TO STAY

Artesia Heritage Inn
209 West Main Street
Artesia, NM 88210
575-748-2552
artesiaheritageinn.com

fectly. The hotel was, in fact, torn down in 1978. The current Hotel Artesia (203 North 2nd Street, Artesia, NM, 88210; 888-746-2066, hotelartesia.com) is the same in name only. The crew could do as they pleased with the hotel as long as they could stand the years of accumulated dust from disuse. For Newton, the hotel became a venue for his struggles with his new physical limitations. He collapses in an elevator shaft, the literal weight of the world too much for his extra-planetary body. The employee at the hotel who rescues him becomes his earthly paramour. Academy Award–winner Candy Clark played the part.

She asks Newton to attend a church service with the townspeople. The scene was filmed at local First Evangelical Presbyterian Church (402 West Grand Avenue, Artesia, NM, 88210). In the scene, Newton draws attention because he doesn't know the words to the hymn of "Jerusalem" and can barely keep up with the service. Although Bowie had early plans to write music for the film, he was not able to deliver on time. His pathetic pantomiming at the service became the only time that Bowie sang on camera or in post-production for the film.

While in Artesia, visit the Artesia Historical Museum and Art Center (505 West Richardson Avenue, Artesia, NM, 88210; 575-748-2390, artesianm.gov/154/Museum-Art-Center), and take a downtown walking tour. Start the walking tour at the Visitor's Center (107 North 1st Street, Artesia, NM, 88211; 575-746-2744, artesiachamber.com). Originally built as a railroad depot, the center is visible in several shots in *The Man Who Fell to Earth*.

SELECTED FILMOGRAPHY

Roeg, Nicolas, dir. *The Man Who Fell to Earth*. USA: Cinema 5 Distributing, 1976. Film.

44

SILVER CITY

To recreate a miner's strike, producers of the 1954 film Salt of the Earth *used real miners and some actual locations near the Empire Mine in Silver City.*

Little Silver City, with its population of under ten thousand, has an unusually controversial history of filmmaking. It was the site of a comeback project for a member of the Hollywood ten, screenwriter Herbert Biberman. He was blacklisted from the film industry and sent to prison for six months in 1950 (see location 27 for New Mexico's connection to another member of this group). His sentence came as a result of the House Un-American Activities Committee (HUAC) hearings, a congressional search for purported Communist activity in the United States. Once released, Biberman wanted to get back to work, but he had more than a few obstacles standing in his way.

Even though the studio system wanted nothing to do with Biberman, he and his partners managed to get a production company off the ground—they had no intention of being intimidated or silenced by HUAC. Looking for writing inspiration, they happened across a mining strike at the Empire Zinc Mine near Silver City, New Mexico.

In 1952, unionized miners at the Empire Zinc Mine protested discriminatory practices against Mexican American employees. Their strike lasted for fifteen months before the parent company, New Jersey Zinc, finally allowed Mexican Americans to receive the same housing benefits and compensation as their white coworkers. For Biberman, and the rest of his company, the struggle en-

Rosa Revueltas and Juan Chacón in *Salt of the Earth* (1954). Courtesy of the Paul Andrew Hutton Collection and Independent Productions.

dured by the miners in Silver City seemed like a tailor-made true story.

Of course, Biberman and his partners ran into trouble almost from the start. The blacklist effectively prohibited them from hiring a union camera crew. But Biberman and his company, ever committed to the rights of workers, refused to find a non-union alternative in California. Fortunately, Biberman had a workaround. He flew to New York and recruited a documentary crew to shoot his narrative film.

For the sake of authenticity, Biberman wanted to shoot in Silver City at the actual mines. He was concerned, though, that he and his crew might have trouble using a publicly accessible location when word of their project reached locals. So Biberman secured a private ranch, but his suspicions proved correct. All across the United States, fear of communism and seemingly sympathetic groups ran high. It didn't surprise Biberman that vigilantes and moral crusaders in Silver City threatened the film.

Residents of Silver City and the surrounding towns weren't the only impediment to the film. Eventually the Federal Bureau of Investigations and execs in Hollywood threw their weight against it. The star of the film, a Mexican national named Rosa Revueltas, was deported, and the film had to be completed with a stand-in.

Even with all the mounting adversity, Biberman managed to finish and release the film. In the midst of the Cold War and fear of communist infiltrators, the film found a small audience and is now regarded as something of a minor classic.

Salt of the Earth was not the first film to use the mines near Silver City for storytelling, although it may be the most dramatic. In 1913 the frontier town attracted director, actor, and all-around luminary Romaine Fielding of the Lubin Southwest Film Company (see location 25 for more information on Fielding). Fielding's brother, while scouting in New Mexico, noticed the huge mines in the Silver City area and told Romaine that they were worth seeing and shooting. Fielding took his brother at his word and made Silver City his hub for a time. Fielding shot in the mines several

HOW TO GET THERE

At the intersection of US Route 180 and New Mexico State Road 90.

WHERE TO STAY

The Murray Hotel
200 W. Broadway Street
Silver City, NM 88061
575-956-9400
murray-hotel.com

WHERE TO EAT

Revel
304 North Bullard Street
Silver City, NM 88061
575-388-4920
eatdrinkrevel.com

times, including one take of a large-scale demolition.

Filmmakers used the mines near Silver City again for the 2005 film *North Country*. The film is a dramatic retelling of a class-action sexual-harassment lawsuit at a working mine in Minnesota. Most of the film was shot in Minnesota, but the underground work was done in Silver City.

The Silver City area has a long mining history, as it is rich with a variety of stones and minerals. Native people mined copper in the area, and the Spanish colonists followed suit when they discovered valuable deposits in 1799. Lead, zinc, gold, and silver mines soon followed all over the area. A number of historic mines still operate in and around Silver City. Some, like the Chino Mine, have produced minerals for years. The Santa Rita del Cobre Mine, a massive copper-pit mine, is visible from New Mexico State Road 152 at the junction with New Mexico State Road 356.

Mineral discoveries in the late 1800s spurred interest in the area, and a tent city arose rapidly in the 1870s. The boomtown garnered a reputation for lawlessness and hosted outlaws like Billy the Kid. The railroad reached Silver City in 1886, solidifying the town's rapid growth. A university soon followed.

The site of the Empire Zinc Mine strike is in what is now Hanover, New Mexico, just a few miles north of the Santa Rita del Cobre Mine on Fiero Road off New Mexico State Road 152. Visible structures from the heyday of the mines include a large head frame, housing, and an old post office. About a hundred people still live in the area, so please be respectful as you explore.

The Silver City Museum (312 West Broadway, Silver City, NM, 88061; 575-538-5921, silvercitymuseum.org), built as the home of a successful prospector in 1881, recaps the local timeline in a historic building. They have rotating exhibits and a collection of Silver City items.

Silver City makes a good base from which to explore the Gila Mountains and their natural and historic parks. The Catwalk Recreation Area (New Mexico State Road 174, near Glenwood, NM, 88039; 575-539-2481, fs.usda.gov/recarea/gila/recarea/?recid =2029) is home to a seemingly impossible metal walkway that stretches along a deep canyon. Part of a late nineteenth-century mining claim, the catwalk was built so that mine workers could service a pipe that provided water to a nearby mill. Slightly farther away, the Gila Cliff Dwellings National Monument (26 Jim Bradford Trail, Mimbres, NM, 88049; 575-536-9461, nps.gov/gicl) is a striking remnant of the Mogollon civilization that features a stone Pueblo built high on a cliffside.

SELECTED FILMOGRAPHY

Biberman, Herbert J., dir. *Salt of the Earth*. USA: Independent Productions, 1954. Film.

Caro, Niki, dir. *North Country*. USA: Warner Bros., 2005. Film.

White Sands National Monument as it appears in the film *White Sands* (1992). Courtesy of Warner Bros.

45

WHITE SANDS

The distinctive gypsum dunes of White Sands appeared in Transformers *in 2007.*

In the first live-action *Transformers* movie, a battalion of American soldiers is chased across the dunes of the Middle East by a mechanical, subterranean threat. Their pursuer is, of course, a robotic alien mimicking a scorpion—a so-called "transformer." The desert it was filmed in, however, was far from the Middle East—it was actually White Sands National Park in New Mexico.

Once the floor of an ancient ocean, the formations at White Sands are the remains of selenite crystals that have been ground into fine white dust and blown into dunes. The result is an expanse of soft, white sands that feel like an out-of-place beach. Some of the dunes reach three stories in height, making the vistas quite impressive.

The gypsum has relatively little value for industrial purposes and, luckily for those wanting to appreciate the beauty of the area, it proved too difficult to mine and ship. So, when calls to make White Sands a National Monument began at the turn of the last century, there was little pushback. White Sands officially became a National Park in 1933 and drew thousands of guests on opening day the following year.

World War II made things stranger. Isolated White Sands National Park got a new neighbor when the one-and-a-quarter-million-acre Alamogordo Bombing and Gunnery Range started operations in 1942. Weapons testing would later force the park to close from time to time because the White Sands Missile Range borders it. The atomic bomb was detonated at the Trinity Site, just sixty miles from White Sands. (The Trinity testing of the "Gadget" was recreated for the television show *Manhattan* but filmed at Bonanza Creek Ranch near Santa Fe.)

The park was the namesake of a 1992 neo-noir mystery thriller starring Willem Defoe and Mickey Rourke in which the film's central villain goes off on a long diatribe about the natural history of White Sands. In the film, a diligent, small-town sheriff played by Defoe goes undercover to find a murderer. The film makes good use of the New Mexico landscape by shooting the state's scenic highlights, including the Rio Grande Gorge, the Santa Fe Plaza, and White Sands.

Much of the *Transformers* work was done at the two military bases near the National Park. *Transformers* and its sequel, *Transformers: Revenge of the Fallen* made extensive use of Holloman Air Force Base. The production built large sets for both films. They also hired hundreds of active airmen to work as extras in the film and made use of one of the base's F22A Raptor jets. The first *Transformers* was the largest film supported by the Department of Defense since *Black Hawk Down* shot five years earlier.

In addition to the major motion-picture and television work at the park, hundreds of commercials and fashion shows feature the sand dunes as a backdrop each year. In 1995, the R&B phenom Boyz II Men shot their music video for "Water Runs Dry" at White Sands. The gypsum sand in the background of the video is unmistakable.

The park is home to a number of trails, all with views of the rolling white dunes. The Interdune Boardwalk Trail makes for a short walk over an elevated esplanade. For a little lon-

HOW TO GET THERE

The park is located on US Route 70 near mile marker 199.

575-479-6124
nps.gov/whsa

Please check operating hours and weather prior to visiting.

WHERE TO STAY

Nearby Alamogordo has several chain motels and hotels.

ger trek, the Backcountry Trail heads into the center of the dunes and is popular with backpackers.

Unexpectedly, sledding might be the top activity in the park. The gift store sells waxed, round saucers, and many of the dunes throughout the park are safe for the sport. Don't be surprised to see hordes of children treating the gypsum like snow in the mountains.

CREW MEMORY

The director wanted to capture the progression of the universe and the human species. He filmed using only natural light. We were in White Sands, and the days were planned down to the minute. The golden hour, when the light stretches over the horizon, was our target. Sunrise and sunset were also highly coveted. For certain shots, the director even thought about the stage of the moon and its effect. When our timing was correct, the natural light reflected off the particles of white sand for miles and miles, and the dunes rose and fell like waves. —*Francheska Bardacke*

SELECTED FILMOGRAPHY

Bay, Michael, dir. *Transformers: Revenge of the Fallen*. USA: Paramount Pictures, 2009. Film.

———. *Transformers: The Movie*. USA: Paramount Pictures, 2007. Film.

Rockhound State Park in *Gas Food Lodging* (1992). Courtesy of IRS Media.

46

DEMING

Independent film history and rockhounding can both be found in Deming.

Part of the Gadsden Purchase of 1883, this fledgling township was named in honor of a railroad investor's wife and functioned as a whistle-stop for years.

Deming's neighbor, Columbus, was the site of Pancho Villa's 1916 raid into the United States during the Mexican Revolution. The raid escalated into a battle with the American Cavalry at the end of which Villa and his troops were driven back into Mexico, but only after they had all but torched Columbus to the ground. Pancho Villa State Park commemorates the event (400 West State Road 9, Columbus, NM, 88029; 575-531-2711, emnrd.state.nm.us/SPD/panchovillastatepark.html).

1954's *Ring of Fear* featured Deming as the background for a traveling circus. Mickey Spillane, better known for his work as a crime novelist than an actor, plays a lightly fictionalized version of himself in this film. In real life, Spillane sold millions of detective novels about a character named Mike Hammer, who lives a bloody and sex-filled existence. Several of his books were made into movies. In *Ring of Fear*, the cinematic Spillane is called in to investigate a murder and sabotage plot that the circus doesn't want the cops to get involved in. Deming provided the space needed to create the life of the circus mystery.

In *Gas Food Lodging* two young women struggle to come of age in a fictional New Mexico town that bares a strong resemblance to Deming. Based on the book titled *Don't Look and It Won't Hurt* by Richard Peck, Fairuza Balk and Ione Skye, both matinee idols of the 1980s and 1990s, play two daughters of a freeway-side restau-

HOW TO GET THERE

Deming can be reached on Interstate 10.

WHERE TO STAY

Deming has several chain motels and hotels.

rant worker. Deming plays their geographic captor, surrounding the angsty teens with bleak isolation. The film was directed by Allison Anders and also stars James Brolin and Donovan Leitch Jr., son of the famed sixties singer.

For the sequel to the reboot of the Rocky franchise, *Creed II*, the title character heads to the desert to reinvigorate his boxing career. The sequence filmed in Deming is an homage to the classic training montages made famous by the original Rocky films.

Deming makes a convenient base to explore some nearby attractions. Rockhound State Park (9880 Stirrup Road SE, Deming, NM, 88030; 575-546-6182, emnrd.state.nm.us/SPD/rockhoundstatepark.html), seen briefly in *Gas Food Lodging*, is just south of Deming. The park is full of semiprecious minerals that interested rockhounds can gather with hand tools. Most of the easy-to-find gems are already combed over, so a little work is required to get a quality souvenir.

Similarly named, but completely different, City of Rocks State Park (327 New Mexico State Road 61, Faywood, NM, 88034; 575-536-2800, emnrd.state.nm.us/SPD/cityofrocksstatepark.html) is a great spot for hiking and bouldering. The park is filled with free-standing stone spires and trails that weave between them.

SELECTED FILMOGRAPHY

Anders, Allison, dir. *Gas Food Lodging*. USA: IRS Media, 1992. Film.

Caple, Steven, Jr., dir. *Creed II*. USA: MGM, 2018. Film.

Grant, James Edward, and William A. Wellman, creators. *Ring of Fear*. USA: Warner Bros., 1954. Film.

47

LORDSBURG AND ENVIRONS

Ghost towns old and new surround this former railroad stop.

Lordsburg sprang up along the Southern Pacific Railroad in 1880 and soon grew into a convenient rest stop along New Mexico State Roads 70 and 80. In the 1960s, Lordsburg boasted several dozen motels, a number of restaurants, and about thirty service stations.

The town's heyday, though, was short lived, as the completion of Interstate 10 rendered their services and motels all but unnecessary. Lordsburg began a slow decline but has recently become a gateway to other ghost towns in the area.

The Shakespeare Ghost Town, although only open to visitors intermittently, is a well-decayed example of a nineteenth-century boomtown. At first, the town was a watering hole known as Mexican Springs. A little later, wagons arrived along the route for the Butterfield Overland Mail service. The discovery of silver in the 1870s brought several decades of growth and activity as well as a new name—Shakespeare. A secondary boom was eventually busted by the 1930s.

Nearby Playas, New Mexico didn't become a ghost town until 1999. Built for employees of the Phelps-

HOW TO GET THERE

Shakespeare Ghost Town
P.O. Box 253
Lordsburg, NM 88045
575-542-9034
shakespeareghostown.com

Shakespeare is open to visitors by appointment only.

WHERE TO STAY

Lordsburg has several chain motels and hotels.

Dodge Corporation, Playas was a master-planned community completed in 1971. The town had a supermarket, tennis courts, a bowling alley, a bank, a community center, and 260 homes. When the value of copper plummeted, though, there wasn't much need for the smelter, and Playas was abandoned.

Playas received a second life when the New Mexico Institute of Mining and Technology purchased it from Phelps-Dodge. They turned the abandoned town into a training center for counter-terrorism, urban warfare, and hostage negotiation. They even expanded Playas and built a replica of an Afghani Village onsite. *Batman v Superman: Dawn of Justice* used the town briefly.

SELECTED FILMOGRAPHY

Snyder, Zack, dir. *Batman v Superman: Dawn of Justice*. USA: Warner Bros., 2016. Film.

48

CARLSBAD CAVERNS

The deep caves at Carlsbad Caverns stood in for a much deeper hole in Journey to the Center of the Earth, *released in 1959 and based on the novel by Jules Verne.*

A designated UNESCO World Heritage Site, Carlsbad Caverns National Park is an intricate web of more than 180 miles of interlinked caves. Inside are spellbinding stalactites, stalagmites, and other formations described as lily pads, ribbons, curtains, and shelves.

Once a massive sponge and algae reef, an uplifting action brought the ancient formation toward the surface of the earth. Hydrogen sulfide leached from the expansive petroleum reservoir at the Permian Basin and mixed with water to create sulfuric acid. Over time, acid at the underground water line ate away at the ancient reef and created hundreds of caverns.

Americans began exploring the caverns around 1898. A few decades later, as popular photographs sparked national interest, the United States Congress made the caves a national monument. The National Park Service added walkways, stairs, and an elevator for easier access to the underground labyrinth and to keep the many tourists from leaving their marks on the place.

Filmmakers arrived at the caverns as early as 1924. The architecture of the caves is perfect for science fiction, and many B films made use of the caves. For the adaptation of H. Rider Haggard's novel *King Solomon's Mines*, filmmakers shot in the Slaughter Canyon Cave. The story follows adventurer Allan Quatermain as he braves the lost civilizations of Africa to find his brother. The novel was a breakout hit in the late nineteenth century and inspired sev-

Deborah Kerr, Richard Carlson, and Stewart Granger in *King Solomon's Mines* (1950). Courtesy of the Paul Andrew Hutton Collection and Metro-Goldwyn Mayer.

eral adaptations. The film featured actual safari footage from Africa along with fanciful scenes from the caverns. Audiences at the time were unaccustomed to this kind of photography, and it made the film something of a visual curiosity and a box-office hit.

A few years later, another adaptation took advantage of the caverns. *Journey to the Center of the Earth*, shot in 1958, used the caverns to bring the imagination of author Jules Verne to life. The big adventure romp follows a group of explorers who follow a treasure map into an unbelievable primordial land. The film crew had to shoot at night because the caverns proved so popular that tourists flooded the caves during the day.

In *Jonathan Livingston Seagull* an unlikely guest visits the caverns and literally flies through it. The film, an adaptation of a novella, follows a seagull as it travels across the country and survives difficult trials. Filmmakers used real seagulls for the footage, and critic Roger Ebert later complained in his review that he couldn't stomach the sight of birds suffering in flight and on screen.

Most visitors access the caverns via a mile-and-a-quarter trail into the "Big Room." Another path of the same length, called the natural entrance trail, goes through the provocatively named Devil's Den. Other parts of the caverns, including Slaughter Canyon, are reachable along a guided ranger tour. The tours are popular, and reservations are necessary.

While seagulls are not usually in residence at the caverns, during the summer Mexican free-tailed bats fly out of the caves en

HOW TO GET THERE

27 Carlsbad Caverns Highway
Carlsbad, NM 88220
575-785-2232
nps.gov/cave

WHERE TO STAY

Nearby Carlsbad has several chain motels and hotels. Over the past few years, the prevalence of oil has turned Carlsbad into something of a boomtown. On occasion, hotel rates can skyrocket.

masse. Rangers hold an evening program to discuss the bats and then watch them in flight from an amphitheater.

For a little fresh air, there are numerous above-ground trails throughout the national park, including some longer backpacking trails. Expect great views of the Guadalupe Mountains and the desert ecosystem in the area.

SELECTED FILMOGRAPHY

Bartlett, Hall, dir. *Jonathan Livingston Seagull*. USA: Paramount Pictures, 1973. Film.

Bennett, Compton, and Andrew Morton, dirs. *King Solomon's Mines*. USA: Metro-Goldwyn Mayer, 1950. Film.

Levin, Henry, dir. *Journey to the Center of the Earth*. USA: Twentieth Century Fox, 1959. Film.

PART VII

ADDITIONAL DESTINATIONS

The J.W. Eaves Movie Ranch (2017).
Photo by Celli Crawford.

NEW MEXICO STUDIOS

Even in New Mexico, the bread and butter of the production process is stage space. Despite the prevalence of so many varied and attractive locations, productions still require a controlled environment where the crew can easily manipulate lighting, sets, and temperature.

New Mexico is home to several professional-quality studios headlined by Q Studios in southern Albuquerque. The three-hundred-thousand-square-foot space at the studio includes eight sound stages, a full suite of offices, a construction mill, and even retail space. Built in 2006, the studio was part of a master planned community at Mesa Del Sol. In 2018, streaming giant Netflix purchased the studio with financial assistance provided by the City of Albuquerque and the state of New Mexico. In exchange, Netflix agreed to spend $1 billion in production expenses over ten years in New Mexico.

Over its ten-year run, Q Studios has hosted some of the largest films in state history, including *Marvel Studios' The Avengers*, *Terminator Salvation*, *Independence Day: Resurgence*, *Sicario*, *The Spirit*, and many others. The studio was also home to long-running television shows like *The Night Shift*, *Breaking Bad*, and *Better Call Saul*.

Although the studio is not open to the public, the roads and landmarks on the way will look familiar. Colloquially called "Snake Road," the southern end of University Boulevard winds through dunes and desert for about six miles after the Rio Bravo exit. The dunes and the overpass are almost an extended backlot to the studio and show up in many films and television shows. Farther down the road, just past the Isleta Amphitheater, Bobby Foster Road is constantly in use by productions. Because the road can be closed to external traffic, it is convenient for productions. Better yet, it has unspoiled views of the Manzano mountains in the distance.

University Boulevard ends at the glass-fronted, Antoine Predock–designed Aperture Center at Mesa del Sol (5700 University Boulevard SE, Albuquerque, NM, 87106), which is also a mainstay for productions. The building hosts a handful of businesses, a small café, and the University of New Mexico's Department of Film and Digital Arts.

On the opposite side of the studio stands the backlot built for *Midnight, Texas*, an NBC television series based on the Charlene Harris paranormal romance novel series. The show lasted only 2 seasons, but NBC Universal returned to the backlot for *The Brave*. The backlot is private property and not open for visitation.

The other major facility in Albuquerque is I-25 Studios on the northern end of town. Once a semiconductor plant, the building was first used as a visiting location and then transitioned into a full-time facility with five hundred thousand square feet of studio space. The television show *In Plain Sight* was an early tenant and took advantage of the sprawling facility by transforming vacant offices and corridors into additional sets. Shows like *Chambers*, *Deputy*, and *The Messengers* followed suit. I-25 Studios is rarely open to the public but is visible from Interstate 25 near the Alameda exit.

Almost directly north on Interstate 25, about fifty miles away, is the Santa Fe Studios. Built in 2011, the facility has two stages, a mill, and office space. The studios hosted *Roswell, New Mexico*; *The Ballad of Buster Scruggs*; *The Ridiculous 6*; and many others. It's not open to the public but is visible from New Mexico State Road 14. It sits right across the street from the Old Main State Penitentiary.

Among the older stages in the state, Greer Garson Studios is located near central Santa Fe. The three stages were initially funded by Garson herself. *Young Guns 2*, *Haywire*, *Wyatt Earp*, and *Legion* all used the Garson. The studio is part of a former college campus facility. At press time, the college is no longer in use.

Several other New Mexico cities have recently completed studios. The Film Las Cruces Studios is seventy-five thousand square feet in size, and the City of Farmington has plans to build a film studio. At press time, the city was evaluating locations but had yet to start construction.

CREW MEMORY

One month after I moved back from Los Angeles, I took my first set production assistant job on *Midnight, Texas*, which was shooting near Q Studios. I didn't even own warm clothes, and I had no idea what to expect in terms of the weather. It was the end of October, and I thought it would be warm all day and night. When it got cold, I had to borrow a scarf, pants, a jacket, and gloves from the costume department. I was doing lockups on the road for four hours for a car stunt scene. My legs stiffened up and my hair froze. Literally. But now I know . . . *—Hattie Brown, Photographer*

CREW MEMORY

I've worked at Albuquerque Studios on various productions over the past several years. I always enjoy working at these studios because I've gotten to know the staff so well, and some of them have become good friends. It's so nice coming to work daily and getting to see friends that have become family over time.

A few years back, while I was working in the costumes department, I ran into the actor Sean Penn. Literally. I was leaving our costumes office with my arms loaded full of shopping bags. My coworkers were talking to me on the way out, so I was focused on their instruction and on not dropping any bags. As I opened the door and walked into the hallway, a group of people were walking past at the same time. I bumped into one person, and I immediately apologized and moved out of the way. As I looked up to see who the gentlemen were, I saw that the man that I had run into was Sean Penn. I was embarrassed and star struck at the same time. I've watched Sean Penn in so many films growing up and am a fan. *—Jessica Clark, Set Decoration Buyer*

HOW TO GET THERE

Q Studios (a.k.a. Albuquerque Studios)
5650 University Boulevard SE
Albuquerque, NM 87106
abqstudios.com

I-25 Studios
9201 Pan American Freeway NE
Albuquerque, NM 87113
i-25studios.com

Santa Fe Studios
1 Santa Fe Studios Road
Santa Fe, NM 87508
santafestudios.com

Garson Studios
1600 St. Michaels Drive
Santa Fe, NM 87505
garsonstudios.com

Film Las Cruces Studios
2100 South Valley Drive
Las Cruces, NM 88005
filmlascruces.com

Studios are secure facilities and are not open to the public unless otherwise noted.

NEW MEXICO THEATERS

The oldest theater in the state was built in the territorial era (1850–1912). Albert Fountain Jr. purchased the building that would become the Fountain Theater in 1905 and then renovated it into a stage-play venue. Fountain was the surviving son of Albert Jennings Fountain, who served as a speaker of the house for the New Mexico House of Representatives. He was also a successful lawyer and newspaperman. In 1896 he disappeared near White Sands, possibly killed by his rival Albert Bacon Fall. Fall would become the architect of the Teapot Dome Scandal, taking bribes to hand over government property to oil drillers. Amazingly, the theater stayed mostly within the Fountain family until 2008. The theater is now operated by the Mesilla Valley Film Society. It screens independent films and hosts special events (2469 Calle De Guadalupe, Mesilla, NM, 88046; 575-524-8287, mesillavalleyfilm.org).

Built about ten years later, the Luna Theater in Clayton features Art Deco styling and a funny winking moon on the marquee. The theater has been lovingly restored by the town of Clayton and updated to play modern films (4 Main Street, Clayton, NM, 88415; 575-374-2712).

Almost the same age, the Shuler Theater in Raton is a showcase venue with 450 seats and a series of Depression-era murals. The theater was restored beginning in the 1960s, and today it is used for live performances (131 North 2nd Street, Raton, NM, 87740; 575-445-4746, shulertheater.com).

The El Morro Theatre in Gallup still plays films with modernized equipment. The theater was built in 1928 with a Spanish Colonial Revival facade. It's owned by the City of Gallup and is used for special events and screenings (207 West Coal Avenue, Gallup, NM, 87301; 505-726-2600, elmorrotheatre.com).

In Santa Fe, the Lensic Performing Arts Center is still the center of cultural events in the City Different. A local merchant built the

The Kimo makes a cameo in *Better Call Saul* (2015–2021). Courtesy of Sony Pictures Television / AMC.

theater in 1931 for films and performances. The theater closed in 1999, but new ownership remodeled the building and reopened it in 2001. The Lensic once again has live performances and film screenings (211 West San Francisco Street, Santa Fe, NM, 87501; 505-988-1234, lensic.org).

The granddaddy of New Mexico theaters is the KiMo Theatre in downtown Albuquerque. Commissioned at the behest of Albuquerque liquor vendor Oreste Bacechi in 1925, architect Carl Boller traveled all over New Mexico in search of inspiration for a grand theater. Boller visited the Navajo Nation and Acoma Pueblo to gather design ideas. The result of his research became the Pueblo Deco theme of the theater. Inside are Navajo swastikas, buffalo skulls, war drums, and funeral canoes. Even the name is derived from Pueblo language words for mountain lions. The theater opened in 1927 and was a landmark along Route 66. The city took possession of the KiMo in the 1970s and restored it for use as a special event space and film venue (423 Central Avenue NW, Albuquerque, NM, 87102; 505-768-3522, cabq.gov/culturalservices/kimo).

Ad for *Convoy* (1978). Courtesy of the Paul Andrew Hutton Collection and United Artists.

A HOLLYWOOD INSIDER ON NEW MEXICO

Nick Guerra, Vice President of Development, Icon

When I told people I was heading to New Mexico for a twelve-week film shoot, the sympathy it elicited made me think I was going to a penitentiary for a stretch that was five times that length. And while it has been a few years since that trip, and my memory is a bit hazy, I think someone did describe the state (and Albuquerque specifically) as a prison sentence. The only virtue that anyone came up with when talking about Albuquerque was Christmas sauce.

Coming from a family that spent two generations on a ranch in New Mexico, I was going to make up my own mind.

My primary purpose for being there was to work on *Blood Father*, a feature directed by Jean-Francois Richet starring Mel Gibson. The movie was the sixth one I had worked on and my first time in Albuquerque. Prior to that I had worked in Boston, New York, Mexico, Texas, and Bulgaria. Every location had its charms, but New Mexico remains one my favorite locations to shoot for a variety of reasons.

CREW

New Mexico is home to a full-service crew who are as high caliber as any I have ever worked with. Across the board, all departments have skilled technicians. To a person, they had an exceptional work ethic. New Mexico can be a hard and unforgiving land with days of extreme heat, high winds, blowing sand, and the occasional rattlesnake sighting. The local crew worked through it all without complaint, and they were never short on hospitality.

LOCATIONS

Albuquerque and its environs were ideal for this particular movie, and while we traveled to approximately ten different locations there seemed to be no shortage of great locations to shoot—trailer parks, hotels, movie theaters, and more—that were easily accessible, unlike shooting in larger cities where every location felt like an ordeal to lock down.

OFF HOURS

I will perpetuate the stereotype of Angelenos as fitness obsessed by mentioning two of my favorite places to train and blow off steam. Del Norte Sports and Wellness (7120 Wyoming Boulevard NE, Suite 8B, Albuquerque, NM, 87109; 505-857-0123, wellbridge .com/sports-and-wellness-del-norte) and Jackson Wink MMA Academy (301 Dr. Martin Luther King Jr. Avenue NE, Albuquerque, NM, 87102; 505-900-3947, jacksonwink.com) are two of the finest gyms I've ever trained at, and both have state-of-the-art facilities with great trainers and friendly clientele.

Once I worked off the stress that comes with filmmaking, I'd usually take a weekly trip to Page 1 Books, a used bookstore with a great selection and a knowledgeable staff. Bring an extra suitcase.

In terms of cuisine, two places are noteworthy: El Pinto (10500 4th Street NW, Albuquerque, NM, 87114; 505-898-1771, elpinto .com), which is pure New Mexican cuisine with its use of Hatch chiles, and the Ranchers Club of New Mexico (1901 University Boulevard NE, Albuquerque, NM, 87102; 505-889 8071, theranch ersclubofnm.com), a steak joint just like you want it, with taxidermied animal heads everywhere and wall-to-wall mahogany.

Albuquerque hosted a Comic Con when I was there. It was no match for San Diego's convention, but it was filled with all of the major comic book imprints, exceptional artists, and Lou Ferrigno!

If time allows, I recommend driving to Santa Fe, a hotbed of art and creativity. The list of writers that live in Santa Fe alone is enough to convince me the city has magical properties. Check out Jean Cocteau Cinema, reopened by George R. R. Martin. Catch a classic movie and maybe get a sighting of everyone's favorite fantasy author and have him sign memorabilia.

My opinion of New Mexico, after a short period of time there, is that it is a place where commerce, art, and recreation combine nicely. The state became, and has remained, a viable and attractive place to shoot thanks to the tax rebate. Beyond the fiscal sense it makes to work there, the solid crews make it a must-consider when planning on shooting either film or television.

A shoot at the Rio Chama (2006).
Photo by Celli Crawford.

ACKNOWLEDGMENTS

This book would not have been possible without the contributions of my fellow New Mexico crew members, many of whom made additions to the text. I've worked out of state and can confidently say that this is the best film-production crew base in the country. Special thanks go to Wolf Schneider and Cyndy McCrossen, who both loaned their expertise on New Mexico locations and film history to this project. They helped me shape the book and added innumerable details that I would have otherwise missed.

Thanks also to Distinguished Professor of History at the University of New Mexico Paul Andrew Hutton, who offered counsel and his vast collection of movie memorabilia.

My gratitude to Alicia Keyes and Bruce Krasnow at the New Mexico Economic Development Department for agreeing to introduce the book and for their enthusiasm.

My family read several drafts of this book and endured countless hours of my complaining about the breadth of the work. Their ears and eyes are always appreciated.

Finally, this book would not exist were it not for Sonia Dickey's suggestion. Thanks to her for presenting me with the idea and for shaping the book into its present form. Thanks to everyone else at the University of New Mexico Press for making this into such a cool project.

Jimmy Stewart and Arthur Kennedy in *The Man from Laramie*, © 1955 (renewed 1983) by Columbia Pictures Industries, Inc. All Rights Reserved. Courtesy of Columbia Pictures and the Paul Andrew Hutton Collection.

NEW MEXICO FILMOGRAPHY

Abrahamson, Lenny, dir. *Frank*. USA: Magnolia Pictures, 2014. Film.

Altman, Robert, dir. *Fool for Love*. USA: Cannon Film Distributors, 1985. Film.

Anders, Allison, dir. *Gas Food Lodging*. USA: IRS Media, 1992. Film.

Anselmo, Reverge, dir. *The Outfitters*. USA: First Look International, 1999. Film.

Arthur, Karen, dir. *The Staircase*. USA: CBS, 1998. TV movie.

Balaban, Bob, dir. *Georgia O'Keeffe*. USA: Sony Pictures Television, 2009. TV movie.

Baldwin, Hunt, and John Coveny, creators. *Longmire*. USA: A+E Networks, 2012-2017. TV series.

Ball, Wes, dir. *Maze Runner: The Scorch Trials*. USA: Twentieth Century Fox, 2015. Film.

Bartlett, Hall. *Jonathan Livingston Seagull*. USA: Paramount Pictures, 1973. Film.

Bay, Michael, dir. *Transformers: Revenge of the Fallen*. USA: Paramount Pictures, 2009. Film.

———. *Transformers: The Movie*. USA: Paramount Pictures, 2007. Film.

Becker, Walt, dir. *Wild Hogs*. USA: Buena Vista Pictures, 2007. Film.

Bennett, Compton, and Andrew Marton, dirs. *King Solomon's Mines*. USA: Metro-Goldwyn-Mayer (MGM), 1950. Film.

Berg, Peter, dir. *Lone Survivor*. USA: Universal Pictures, 2013. Film.

Beumer, Antoinette, dir. *Jackie*. USA: Tribeca Film, 2012. Film.

Biberman, Herbert J., dir. *Salt of the Earth*. USA: Independent Productions, 1954. Film.

Blechynden, Frederik, camera. *Indian Day School*. USA: Thomas A. Edison, Inc, 1898. Video. https://www.loc.gov/item/00564534.

Bouchareb, Rachid, dir. 2014; *Two Men in Town*. USA: Coen Media Group, 2015. Film.

Branagh, Kenneth, dir. *Thor*. USA: Paramount Pictures, 2011. Film.

Brooks, Richard, dir. *Bite the Bullet*. USA: Columbia Pictures, 1975. Film.

Butler, Robert, dir. *Scandalous John*. USA: Buena Vista Distribution Company, 1971. Film.

Buxbaum, Evan, dir. *Sun Belt Express*. USA: MarVista Entertainment, 2014. Film.

Cain, Christopher, dir. *Young Guns*. USA: Twentieth Century Fox, 1988. Film.

Caple, Jr., Steven, dir. *Creed II*. USA: MGM, 2018. Film.

Caro, Niki, dir. *North Country*. USA: Warner Bros., 2005. Film.

Carpenter, John, dir. *Ghosts of Mars*. USA: Screen Gems, 2001. Film.

———. *Vampires*. USA: Columbia Pictures, 1998. Film.

Catlin, Sam, Evan Goldberg, and Seth Rogen, creators. *Preacher*. USA: American Movie Classics (AMC), 2016–2019. TV series.

Coen Brothers, dirs. *The Ballad of Buster Scruggs*. USA: Netflix Studios, 2017. Film.

———. *No Country for Old Men*. USA: Miramax, 2007. Film.

———. *True Grit*. USA: Paramount Pictures, 2010. Film.

Coolidge, Greg, dir. *Employee of the Month*. USA: Lionsgate, 2006. Film.

Cooper, Scott, dir. *Crazy Heart*. USA: Fox Searchlight Pictures, 2009. Film.

Coraci, Frank, dir. *The Ridiculous* 6. USA: Netflix Studios, 2015. Film.

Corman, Roger, dir. *Gas!—Or—It Became Necessary to Destroy the World in Order to Save It*. USA: American International Pictures (AIP), 1970. Film.

Cretton, Destin Daniel, dir. *The Glass Castle*. USA: Lionsgate, 2017. Film.

Croll, Tony, Andrew Glassman, and Jason Raff, dirs. *Three Wishes*. USA: Season 1, episode 2, "Clovis, New Mexico." 2005. Aired on September 30, 2005, on NBC.

Crowley, John, dir. *The Goldfinch*. USA: Amazon Studios, 2019. Film.

Donaldson, Roger, dir. *White Sands*. USA: Warner Bros., 1992. Film.
Downey, Robert, Sr., dir. *Greaser's Palace*. USA: Cinema 5 Distributing, 1972. Film.
Douglas, Gordon, dir. *Only the Valiant*. USA: Warner Bros., 1951. Film.
Ellis, Kirk, producer. *Into the West*. USA: TNT/Dreamworks Television, 2005. TV series.
English, John, dir. *Sons of New Mexico*. USA: Columbia Pictures, 1949. Film.
Eubank, William, dir. *The Signal*. USA: Focus Features, 2014. Film.
Evans, Justin Eugene, dir. *A Lonely Place for Dying*. USA: Humble Magi, 2009. Film.
Eyre, Chris, dir. *A Thief of Time*. USA: Public Broadcasting Service (PBS), 2004. Film.
Favreau, Jon, dir. *Cowboys & Aliens*. USA: Universal Studios, 2011. Film.
Fergus, Mark, dir. 2006; *First Snow*. USA: Sony Pictures Home Entertainment, 2007. DVD.
Ficarra, Glenn, and John Requa, dirs. *Whiskey Tango Foxtrot*. USA: Paramount Pictures, 2016. Film.
Flicker, Theodore J., dir. *Up in the Cellar*. USA: American International Pictures (AIP), 1970. Film.
Florey, Robert, dir. *Desert Song*. USA: Warner Bros., 1943. Film.
Ford, John, dir. *The Grapes of Wrath*. USA: Twentieth Century Fox, 1940. Film.
Foster, Lewis, dir. *El Paso*. USA: Paramount Pictures, 1949. Film.
Franklin, Carl, dir. *Bless Me, Ultima*. USA: Arenas Entertainment, 2012. Film.
Frears, Stephen, dir. *The Hi-Lo Country*. USA: Gramercy Pictures, 1998. Film.
Friedkin, William, dir. *Sorcerer*. USA: Universal Pictures, 1977. Film.
Fuglsig, Nicolai, dir. *12 Strong*. USA: Warner Bros., 2018. Film.
Gaghan, Stephen, dir. *Gold*. USA: TWC-Dimension, 2016. Film.
Gillespie, Craig, dir. *Fright Night*. USA: Walt Disney Studios Motion Pictures, 2011. Film.

Gilligan, Vince, creator. *Breaking Bad*. USA: American Movie Classics (AMC), 2008–2013. TV series.

Gilligan, Vince, and Peter Gould, creators. *Better Call Saul*. USA: American Movie Classics (AMC), 2015–. TV series.

Glazer, Mitch, dir. *Passion Play*. USA: Image Entertainment, 2010. Film.

Grant, James Edward, and William A. Wellman, creators. *Ring of Fear*. USA: Warner Bros., 1954. Film.

Green, Alfred E., dir. *Four Faces West*. USA: United Artists, 1948. Film.

Griffith, D. W., dir. *A Pueblo Legend*. USA: Biograph Company, 1912. Film.

Haggis, Paul, dir. *In the Valley of Elah*. USA: Warner Independent Pictures, 2007. Film.

Harris, Ed, dir. *Appaloosa*. USA: Warner Brothers, 2008. Film.

Hathaway, Henry, dir. *Shoot Out*. USA: Universal Pictures, 1971. Film.

———. *Sundown*. USA: United Artists, 1941. Film.

Hellman, Monte, dir. *Two-Lane Blacktop*. USA: Universal Pictures, 1971. DVD.

Heslov, Grant, dir. *The Men Who Stare at Goats*. USA: BBC Films, 2009. Film.

Hill, Terence, dir. 1991; *Lucky Luke*. USA: A-Pix Entertainment, 2000. DVD.

———. *Botte di Natale*. Italy: Rialto Films, 1994. Film.

Hiller, Arthur, dir. *Outrageous Fortune*. USA: Buena Vista Pictures, 1987. Film.

Hoffman, Michael, dir. *Gambit*. USA: CBS Films, 2012. Film.

Hooper, Jerry, dir. *The Atomic City*. USA: Paramount Pictures, 1952. Film.

Hopper, Dennis, and Peter Fonda, dirs. *Easy Rider*. USA: Columbia Pictures, 1969. DVD.

Howard, Ron, dir. *The Missing*. USA: Columbia Pictures, 2003. Film.

Hughes Brothers, dir. *The Book of Eli*. USA: Warner Bros., 2010. Film.

Hyams, Peter, dir. *2010*. USA: Metro-Goldwyn-Mayer (MGM), 1984. Film.

Iñárritu, Alejandro G., dir. *21 Grams*. USA: Focus Features, 2003. Film.

Irwin, Jack, dir. *White Renegade*. USA: Jack Irwin Productions (as Carlsbad Productions), Weiss Brothers Artclass Pictures, 1931. Film.

Isaacs, Brad, dir. *A West Texas Children's Story*. USA: Thunder Bay Pictures, West Texas New Mexico Films, and WolfGang Cinema, 2007. Film.

Johnson, Lamont, dir. *A Gunfight*. USA: Paramount Pictures, 1971. Film.

Jones, Tommy Lee, dir. *The Homesman*. USA: Roadside Attractions, Saban Films, 2014. Film.

Jordan, Tony, creator. *Crash*. USA: Red Planet Pictures, 2009–2010. TV series.

Judah, Jeff, and Gabe Sachs, creators. *The Night Shift*. USA: National Broadcasting Company (NBC), 2014–2016. TV series.

Kasdan, Lawrence, dir. *Silverado*. USA: Columbia Pictures, 1985. Film.

———. *Wyatt Earp*. USA: Warner Bros., 1994. Film.

Kazan, Elia, dir. *The Sea of Grass*. USA: Metro-Goldwyn-Mayer (MGM), 1947. Film.

Kennedy, Burt, dir. *The Good Guys and the Bad Guys*. USA: Warner Bros., Seven Arts, 1969. Film.

Kim, Jee-woon, dir. *The Last Stand*. USA: Lionsgate, 2013. Film.

Kormákur, Baltasar, dir. *2 Guns*. USA: Universal Pictures, 2013. Film.

Kosinski, Joseph, dir. *Only the Brave*. USA: Columbia Pictures, 2017. Film.

Laughlin, Tom, dir. *Billy Jack*. USA: Warner Bros., 1971. Film.

Lawrence, Marc, dir. *Did You Hear About the Morgans?* USA: Columbia Pictures, 2009. Film.

Lee, Ang, dir. *Brokeback Mountain*. USA: Universal Pictures, 2005. Film.

LeRoy, Mervyn, dir. *Without Reservations*. USA: RKO Radio Pictures, 1946. Film.

Levin, Henry, dir. *Journey to the Center of the Earth*. USA: Twentieth Century Fox, 1959. Film.

Lowry, Dick, dir. *Last Stand at Saber River*. USA: TNT, 1997. TV movie.

Lupino, Ida. *The Trouble with Angels*. USA: Columbia Pictures, 1966. Film.

———. *Where Angels Go, Trouble Follows*. USA: Columbia Pictures, 1968. Film.

Mackenzie, David, dir. *Hell or High Water*. USA: CBS Films, 2016. Film.

Mangold, James, dir. *3:10 to Yuma*. USA: Lionsgate, 2007. Film.

———. *Logan*. USA: Twentieth Century Fox, 2017. Film.

Maples, David, creator. *In Plain Sight*. USA: USA Network, 2008–2012. TV series.

Marin, Edwin L., dir. *Raton Pass*. USA: Warner Bros., 1951. Film.

Marshall, George, dir. *Fancy Pants*. USA: Paramount Pictures, 1950. Film.

———. *Valley of the Sun*. USA: RKO Radio Pictures, 1942. Film.

McCahon, Robert, dir. *Running Wild*. USA: Golden Circle Films, 1973. Film.

McFarlane, Seth, dir. *A Million Ways to Die in the West*. USA: Universal Pictures, 2014. Film.

McG, dir. *Terminator Salvation*. USA: Warner Bros., 2009. Film.

Medak, Peter, dir. *Pontiac Moon*. USA: Paramount Pictures, 1994. Film.

Mendes, Sam, dir. *Jarhead*. USA: Universal Pictures, 2005. Film.

Merhige, E. Elias, dir. *Suspect Zero*. USA: Paramount Pictures, 2004. Film.

Meyers, Dave, dir. *The Hitcher*. USA: Rogue Pictures, 2007. Film.

Milius, John, dir. *Red Dawn*. USA: MGM/UA Entertainment Company, 1984. Film.

Millar, Stuart, dir. *When the Legends Die*. USA: Twentieth Century Fox, 1972. Film.

Miller, David, dir. *Lonely Are the Brave*. USA: Universal Pictures, 1962. Film.

Miller, Logan, and Noah Miller, dirs. *Sweetwater*. USA: ARC Entertainment, 2013. Film.

Montgomery, Robert, dir. *Ride the Pink Horse*. USA: Universal Pictures, 1947. Film.

Moreau, David, and Xavier Palud, dirs. *The Eye*. USA: Lionsgate, 2008. Film.

Morse, Richardson, dir. 1972; *House Made of Dawn*. USA: [limited release], 1972. Film.

Morse, Terry O., dir. *Unknown World*. USA: Lippert Pictures, 1951. Film.

Mottola, Greg, dir. *Paul*. USA: Universal Pictures, 2011. Film.

Murphy, Geoff, dir. *Young Guns II*. USA: Twentieth Century Fox, 1990. Film.

Neveldine, Mark, and Brian Taylor, dirs. *Gamer*. USA: Lionsgate, 2009. Film.

Newman, Joseph M., dir. *Fort Massacre*. USA: United Artists, 1958. Film.

Newman, Kyle, dir. *Fanboys*. USA: Metro-Goldwyn-Mayer, Third Rail Releasing, Comedy Central, 2009. Film.

Niblo, Fred, dir. *Way Out West*. USA: Metro-Goldwyn-Mayer, 1930. Film.

Niccol, Andrew, dir. *Good Kill*. USA: IFC Films, 2014. Film.

———. *The Host*. USA: Open Road Films, 2013. Film.

Nichols, Mike, dir. *Silkwood*. USA: Twentieth Century Fox, 1983. Film.

———. *The Fortune*. USA: Columbia Pictures, 1975. Film.

Nirmalakhandan, Rajeev, dir. *Odd Way Home*. USA: Breaking Glass Pictures, 2014. Film.

Norton, Bill, dir. *Gargoyles*. USA: CBS, 1972. TV movie.

O'Connor, Gavin, dir. *Jane Got a Gun*. USA: The Weinstein Company, 2015. Film.

Owusu-Breen, Monica, Eric C. Charmelo, and Nicole Snyder, creators. *Midnight, Texas*. USA: National Broadcasting Company (NBC), 2017–2018. TV series.

Peckinpah, Sam, dir. *Convoy*. USA: United Artists, 1978. Film.
Pfister, Wally, dir. *Transcendence*. USA: Alcon Entertainment, Warner Bros., 2014. Film.
Phillips, Todd, dir. *Due Date*. USA: Warner Bros., 2010. Film.
Pillsbury, Sam, dir. *Into the Badlands*. USA: USA Network, 1991. Film.
Polish, Michael, dir. *The Astronaut Farmer*. USA: Warner Bros., 2006. Film.
Post, Ted, dir. *Hang 'Em High*. USA: United Artists, 1968. Film.
Pratt, Alexandra, dir. *The Trailblazer*. USA: [limited release], 1997. Film.
Ramis, Harold, dir. *Year One*. USA: Columbia Pictures, 2009. Film.
Range, Gabriel, dir. *Outlaw Prophet: Warren Jeffs*. USA: Lifetime Television, 2014. TV movie.
Rawlins, John, dir. *Fort Defiance*. USA: United Artists, 1951. Film.
———. *Sudan*. USA: Universal Pictures, 1945. Film.
Redford, Robert, dir. *The Milagro Beanfield War*. USA: Universal Pictures, 1988. Film.
Reed, Carol, dir. *Flap*. USA: Warner Bros., 1970. Film.
Reeves, Matt, dir. *Let Me In*. USA: Overture Films, Relativity Media, 2010. Film.
Reitman, Ivan, dir. *Twins*. USA: Universal Pictures, 1988. Film.
Rhodes, Hue, dir. *Saint John of Las Vegas*. USA: IndieVest Pictures, 2009. Film.
Richet, Jean-François, dir. *Blood Father*. USA: Lionsgate Premiere, 2014. Film.
Roach, Jay, dir. *Game Change*. USA: HBO Films, 2012. Film.
Rosenberg, Stuart, dir. *Pocket Money*. USA: First Artists, 1972. Film.
Ross, Matt, dir. *Captain Fantastic*. USA: Universal Pictures Home Entertainment, 2015. Film.
Rydell, Mark, dir. *The Cowboys*. USA: Warner Bros., 1972. Film.
Sapochnik, Miguel, dir. *Finch*. USA: Universal Pictures, 2021, Film.
Schertzinger, Victor, dir. *Redskin*. USA: Paramount Pictures, 1929. Film.
Seaton, George, dir. *Showdown*. USA: Universal Pictures, 1973. Film.

Segal, Peter, dir. *The Longest Yard*. USA: Paramount Pictures, 2005. Film.

Shaw, Sam, creator. *Manhattan*. USA: WGN America, 2014–2015. TV series.

Sheridan, Jim, dir. *Brothers*. USA: Lionsgate, 2009. Film.

Snyder, Zack, dir. *Batman v Superman: Dawn of Justice*. USA: Warner Bros., 2016. Film.

Soderbergh, Steven, dir. *Haywire*. USA: Relativity Media, 2011. Film.

———. *Traffic*. USA: USA Films, 2000. Film.

Sommers, Stephen, dir. *Odd Thomas*. USA: Image Entertainment, 2013. Film.

Sonnenfeld, Barry, dir. *Wild Wild West*. USA: Warner Bros., 1999. Film.

Spielberg, Steven, dir. *Indiana Jones and the Kingdom of the Crystal Skull*. USA: Paramount Pictures, 2008. Film.

———. *Indiana Jones and the Last Crusade*. USA: Paramount Pictures, 1989. Film.

Stern, Joshua Michael, creator. *Graves*. USA: Epix, 2016–2017. TV series.

———. *Swing Vote*. USA: Walt Disney Studios Motion Pictures, 2008. Film.

Stewart, Scott, dir. *Legion*. USA: Screen Gems, 2010. Film.

Stockwell, John, and Paulette Victor-Lifton, dirs. *Seal Team 6: The Raid on Osama bin Laden*. USA: National Geographic Channel, 2012. TV movie.

Stone, Oliver, dir. *Natural Born Killers*. USA: Warner Bros., 1994. Film.

Sturges, John, dir. *The Hallelujah Trail*. USA: United Artists, 1965. Film.

Taccone, Jorma, dir. *MacGruber*. USA: Rogue, Universal Pictures, 2010. Film.

Talalay, Rachel, dir. *Tank Girl*. USA: United Artists, 1995. Film.

Tennant, Andy, dir. *Fools Rush In*. USA: Columbia Pictures, 1997. Film.

Thompson, Donald W., dir. *The Prodigal Planet*. USA: Mark IV Pictures Inc., 1983. Film.

Thompson, J. Lee, dir. *The White Buffalo*. USA: United Artists, 1977. Film.

Thornton, Billy Bob, dir. *All the Pretty Horses*. USA: Sony Pictures, 2000. Film.

Thurber, Rawson Marshall, dir. *We're the Millers*. USA: New Line Cinema, 2013. Film.

Trikonis, Gus, dir. *The Evil*. USA: New World Pictures, 1978. Film.

Turman, Lawrence, dir. *Second Thoughts*. USA: Universal Pictures, Associated Film Distribution, 1983. Film.

Underwood, Ron, dir. *Speechless*. USA: Metro-Goldwyn-Mayer (MGM), 1994. Film.

———. *City Slickers*. USA: Columbia Pictures, 1991. Film.

Vadim, Roger, dir. *And God Created Woman*. USA: Lionsgate, 1987. Film.

Verbinski, Gore, dir. *The Lone Ranger*. USA: Walt Disney Pictures, 2013. Film.

Vidor, King, dir. *The Texas Rangers*. USA: Paramount Pictures, 1936. Film.

Villeneuve, Denis, dir. *Sicario*. USA: Lionsgate, 2015. Film.

Wacks, Jonathan, dir. *Powwow Highway*. USA: Warner Bros., 1989. Film.

Walsh, Raoul, dir. *A Distant Trumpet*. USA: Warner Bros., 1964. Film.

Waugh, Ric Roman, dir. *Shot Caller*. USA: Saban Films, 2017. Film.

Whedon, Joss, dir. *Marvel Studios' The Avengers*. USA: Marvel Studios, 2012. Film.

White, Susanna, dir. *Woman Walks Ahead*. USA: A24, Creative Artists Agency, 2017. Film.

Wilder, Billy, dir. *Ace in the Hole*. USA: Paramount Pictures, 1951. Film.

Wiles, Gordon, dir., and Mark Miller, writer. 1974; *Ginger in the Morning*. USA: Miracle Pictures, 2003. DVD.

Wincer, Simon, dir. *Comanche Moon*. USA: Sony Pictures Home Entertainment, 2008. Film.

Wingard, Adam, dir. *The Guest*. USA: Picturehouse, 2014. Film.

Wise, Robert, dir. *Two Flags West*. USA: Twentieth Century Fox, 1950. Film.

Young, Robert M., dir. *The Ballad of Gregorio Cortez*. USA: Embassy Pictures, 1982. Film.

Zemeckis, Robert, dir. *Contact*. USA: Warner Bros., 1997. Film.

BIBLIOGRAPHY

American Film Institute, pub. "Butch and Sundance: The Early Days (1979)." *AFI Catalog of Feature Films, the First 100 Years 1893–1993*, [2019]. http://catalog.afi.com/Catalog/MovieDetails/56140.

Armijo, John Raymond, ed. *Movies Made in New Mexico, 1898–1999*. Santa Fe, NM: New Mexico Film Office, New Mexico Economic Development Department, 1999.

———. "Early Filmmaking in Meadow City." . Santa Fe, NM: New Mexico Film Office, New Mexico Economic Development Department, undated.

Berg, Jeff. *Historic Movie Theatres of New Mexico*. Charleston, SC: History, 2018.

———. *New Mexico Filmmaking*. Charleston, SC: History, 2015.

Bessman, Jim. "The Oscar-Nominated Music of 'The Ballad of Buster Scruggs.'" Centerline News, February 10, 2019. https://www.centerline.news/single-post/2019/02/11/The-Oscar-nominated-music-of-The-Ballad-of-Buster-Scruggs.

Biberman, Herbert. *Salt of the Earth: The Story of a Film*. New York: Harbor Electronic Publ., 2003.

Boggs, Johnny D. *Billy the Kid on Film, 1911–2012*. Jefferson, NC: McFarland, 2013.

Bowman, Jon, ed. *100 Years of Filmmaking in New Mexico*. Santa Fe, NM: New Mexico Department of Tourism, 1998.

Cather, Willa. *Death Comes for the Archbishop*. New York: Vintage Books, 1990.

Chanko, Kenneth M. "Behind the scenes of "City Slickers"—EW goes out West with the executive-producer and star Billy Crystal," *Entertainment Weekly*, June 21, 1991.

Escutia, Sondra. "Hollywood 'Transforms' Holloman Yet Again." *Holloman Air Force Base Newsletter*, June 26, 2009. https://www.holloman.af.mil/Article-Display/Article/318051/hollywood-transforms-holloman-yet-again.

Finley, Dave. "Hollywood Comes to Socorro: Filming *Contact* at the VLA." *Dave Finley N1IRZ*, 1997. https://qsl.net/n1irz/contact.html.

Gaberscek, Carlo, and Kenny Stier. *In Search of Western Movie Sites*. Eureka, CA: Jerry Schneider Enterprises, LLC., 2014.

Gilligan, Vince, speaker. "Vince Gilligan on the Origins of Breaking Bad." *Conan on TBS*. You Tube video. Posted by Team Coco, Aug. 8, 2012. https://www.youtube.com/watch?v=PKttjlCoLzU.

Gomez, Adrian. "Ranch Tour Shares Its Rich History of Filmmaking." *Albuquerque Journal* (Albuquerque, NM), October 17, 2010.

Hill, Logan. "Fall Preview: Gallows Humor." *New York Magazine*, August 24, 2007. https://nymag.com/guides/fallpreview/2007/movies/36621.

Hillerman, Tony. *Coyote Waits*. New York: Harper Torch, 2009.

Merron, Jeff. "Real vs. Reel: The Longest Yard." *ESPN.com*, June 6, 2005. http://www.espn.com/espn/page2/story?page=merron/050613.

Movie Locations of the Great Southwest. movies.nm-unlimited2.net

Movie-locations.com

Murray, John A. *Cinema Southwest: An Illustrated Guide to the Movies and Their Locations*. Flagstaff, AZ: Northland Publishing, 2000.

Nacho Video. "David Bowie is The Man Who Fell to Earth." You Tube video. Posted on October 15, 2017. https://youtube.com/watch?v=dP8ncgc3nG4.

Nemiroff, Peter. "Peter Berg and Marcus Luttrell Talk LONE SURVIVOR, Cast and Crew Dedication, Making the Movie for the Right Reasons, Honoring Lives Lost, and More." *Collider*, December 19, 2013.

Nichols, John. *Dancing on the Stones: Selected Essays*. Albuquerque: University of New Mexico Press, 2000.

The Public Library, Albuquerque and Bernalillo County. "Filmed in New Mexico." abqlibrary.org/filmedinnm

Rafferty, Liz. "*Breaking Bad* Turns 10: An Oral History of the Pilot." *TV Guide*, January 19, 2018. tvguide.com/news/features /breaking-bad-pilot-oral-history-10th-anniversary.

Schicken, Richard. *Clint Eastwood: A Biography*. New York: Vintage Books, 1997.

Seals, David. *The Powwow Highway: A Novel*. Albuquerque: University of New Mexico Press, 2014.

Sikov, Ed. *On Sunset Boulevard: The Life and Times of Billy Wilder*. Jackson, MI: University Press of Mississippi, 2017.

Svetkey, Benjamin. "Making Contact: The Story Behind the Controversial Space Odyssey." *Entertainment Weekly*, July 18, 1997.

Tatum, Stephen. *Inventing Billy the Kid: Visions of the Outlaw in America, 1881–1981*. Albuquerque: University of New Mexico Press, 1982.

Warner, Denise. "Breaking Bad Recap: To'hajiilee." *Entertainment Weekly*, September 09, 2013. https://ew.com/recap/breaking -bad-season-5-episode-13-tohajiilee.

Wilder, Billy, Cameron Crowe, and Karen Lerner. *Conversations with Wilder*. New York: Knopf, 2001.

Winkler, Peter. *Dennis Hopper: The Wild Ride of a Hollywood Rebel*. Fort Lee, NJ: Barricade Books, 2011.

INDEX OF FILMS AND TELEVISION SHOWS

Page numbers in italic text indicate illustrations.